THE ROMANTIC ENLIGHTENMENT

THE ROMANTIC ENLIGHTENMENT

Geoffrey Clive

MERIDIAN BOOKS, INC. *New York*

GEOFFREY CLIVE

Geoffrey Clive was born in Berlin, Germany, on September 22, 1927. He came to the United States at an early age, and was educated at Colgate and Harvard, where he received his Ph.D. in philosophy in 1953. Mr. Clive has taught at Harvard, the universities of Delaware, Connecticut, and Arkansas, and is now assistant professor of philosophy at Clark University. He is co-editor (with William Kimmel) of an anthology, DIMENSIONS OF FAITH: CONTEMPORARY PROPHETIC PROTESTANT THEOLOGY.

Portions of this book—in different form—appeared in JOURNAL OF RELIGION, MUSIC AND LETTERS, DELAWARE NOTES, LUTHERAN QUARTERLY, *and* HARVARD THEOLOGICAL REVIEW.

M

AN ORIGINAL MERIDIAN BOOK
Published by Meridian Books, Inc. February 1960
First printing January 1960

ACKNOWLEDGMENTS

I feel indebted to the following friends and colleagues for most helpful criticism and suggestions: Dean Samuel H. Miller and Professor James Luther Adams of the Harvard Divinity School; Professor James Barnett of the University of Connecticut; Professor Hans Meyerhoff of U.C.L.A.; Professor Richard Kroner; and Professor Walter Kirchner of the University of Delaware. I owe special thanks to Professor William Kimmel of Hunter College, whose intellectual catholicity and understanding of the great composers are felicitously contagious. And I am particularly grateful to Professors John Wild and Harry Austryn Wolfson of Harvard University for encouragement and support. Professor Sydney Ahlstrom of the Yale Divinity School must take some responsibility for my theological awareness. I am grateful to numerous students and associates for bits of inspiration and advice. Mr. Tilton Barron and the staff of the Clark University Library have been consistently helpful. To my editor, Aaron Asher, I am grateful for his assistance in transforming my manuscript into a book. Thanks are also due to my brother, John Clive, who read the manuscript and made many helpful suggestions, and to Paul Eisenberg, who assisted me with the proof-reading and the index. And without the good will of Elma S. Leavis it is questionable whether the obscurities of my handwriting would ever have been relieved. I alone am responsible for all errors.

G. C.

September 14, 1959

CONTENTS

Preface: The Uses of Kierkegaard

When David Swenson at the University of Minnesota and Reinhold Niebuhr at Union Theological Seminary introduced him to their students in the 1930's, Kierkegaard was practically unknown in the English-speaking world. Since then the situation has changed radically: today, with Nietzsche's, Marx's, and Freud's, his work ranks as seminal for the understanding of modern consciousness and intellectual life. Scarcely a study of the history of ideas since the Enlightenment will now appear which neglects to deal with Kierkegaard (usually in some detail) and the implications of his authorship. This mercurial change of reputation from neglect to something bordering on popularity is due in considerable measure to the uneasiness of our times in which so many are fascinated by genuine presentiments of their sickness and decline.

Expositions of Kierkegaard (omitting here the purely biographical approach) tend to fall into three chief categories: the psychological, the ecclesiological, and the critical. In the first, he is a "literary" psychologist like Shakespeare or Dostoevsky, anticipating if not going beyond the insights into motivation of the psychoanalytic schools. In the second, he is placed next to Cardinal Newman as the outstanding apologist for the Christian faith in the nineteenth century, who ingeniously demolished the idols of materialism and German idealism. Finally, he has influenced and been used to buttress their respective positions by thinkers as far apart as Ortega and Wittgenstein. Kierkegaard the prophet and critic of "mass society" has become especially respectable in recent thought.

Nothing is more commonplace than to condemn "special pleading" and at the same time to reiterate that matters always are and should be looked at from diverse "points of view." One might add here that "balanced presentations" of a great thinker are apt to be unrewarding and dull, while tendentious accounts, their dangerous one-sidedness apart, reveal more about the interpreter than his subject. In any event, the assumptions of objective methodological inquiry are at least as vulnerable as those of "intuition." Actually the latter by being easily recognized will only fool those predisposed to self-deception; whereas the former, by virtue of their "scientific" authority, often exercise a hidden and intransigent power. The alert and honest reader of Kierkegaardian dialectic will soon spot the absurdity of any simple interpretation. On the other hand, he may have far greater difficulty disputing the theologian who on the basis of Kierkegaard's planned Christian authorship disallows any but Christian criticism of his work, as if interpretation of a rich body of thought should be limited a priori to the discernible intention of its author.

In the first place it is absolutely essential to distinguish a writer's books from what he himself remarked about them. Usually, it is safe to generalize, his books are far more significant than his comments on them. It is doubtful whether the latter would have survived without the former. What is interesting about Kierkegaard is not primarily his explicit self-interpretation or his reflections on his complicated authorship, but the works themselves with all their ambiguity and tension. Secondly, it is just as necessary to distinguish the transparent meaning of a body of work from its historical influence and fortunes. A new interpretation, far from being a distortion of the original, can represent an authentic realization of a previously neglected but real possibility. No writer is the master of his work in the sense that he can foresee or control all the eclipses, revivals, and different functions it may come to serve. The legitimacy of these, to be sure, is always open for inspection. But it is as ill-advised to ignore the potentialities of important thought as to overlook what it initially meant. So far as Kierkegaard is concerned, the fact that he regarded himself as a religious thinker must never be obscured, yet it does not follow as a corollary that his categories from the very beginning had not a far wider than Christian significance. Whatever his intentions may have been (and they certainly were anything but clear cut), the historical Kierkegaard is no mere theologian. Like Pascal he has entered the main stream of Western thought, hence is subject to the vicissitudes of history. The Kierkegaard of Rome or of the "New Wittenberg" (Basel) embodies a truth as limited as the Kierkegaard of Heidegger or Sartre. That so many articulate minds in the twentieth century have been sincerely convinced of finding in Kierkegaard's writings whatever they were looking for, is in itself highly relevant to their "contemporaneousness." The influence of such a mind should not be equated with the destination of a sealed railroad car. The no longer "new" critics encouraged this nonsense in setting out to "exhaust" a text once and for all.

This is not a book about Kierkegaard. Nevertheless, were it not for his writings, it would not have been possible. Without sharing his total vision of things—though there is much in it that appeals to me—I am using selected key concepts in order to elucidate a number of vital issues in post-Enlightenment thought. In short, I hold that no little part of the greatness of Kierkegaard lies in his categories and their application both in width and in depth. *The daemonic, subjectivity, the leap, the sickness unto death, the offense, the teleological suspension of the ethical, dehumanization*•—these are instruments of thinking about culture and society since the Enlightenment which, in my opinion, are singularly suggestive and illuminating. What follows is the test of this contention. In the meantime it may be well for the reader to remember that there are many ways of connecting facts and events, and that even the most successful description of its kind will unavoidably be limited by its own assumptions. By success here I mean fundamentally nothing more than shedding light.

• Although, to my knowledge, Kierkegaard never used this term himself, its connotation of overcivilization coincides perfectly with his category of the aesthetic mode of existence.

TO MY PARENTS

Mathematicians who are only mathematicians have exact minds, provided all things are explained to them by means of definitions and axioms; otherwise they are inaccurate and insufferable, for they are only right when the principles are quite clear. And men of intuition who are only intuitive cannot have the patience to reach to first principles of things speculative and conceptual, which they have never seen in the world, and which are altogether out of the common.

Blaise Pascal, *Pensées*

Apparently, then, there is a profound truth in the old saying: "No one contends with God except God Himself." For if there is a God, those Promethean powers which antagonize Him must in some manner be ordained by Him; they must be understood as His most imposing and awe-inspiring manifestation. And is it not precisely the same fundamental principles of ethics and religion, the ideals of truth, freedom, and brotherly love, by which even this insurrection against religion is inspired in the soul of modern man?

Erich Frank, *Philosophical Under-standing and Religious Truth*

The road leads from reason fulfilled in faith through reason without faith to reason filled with demonic-destructive faith.

Paul Tillich, *The Dynamics of Faith*

THE ROMANTIC ENLIGHTENMENT

Introduction:
Ambiguities in Enlightenment Life and Thought

For John Wesley man was spirit; in "the revolt of the masses" he became a commodity. Elements of what transpired between these two extreme views of him constitute the theme of this study. More concretely, it is an inquiry into changes in Western feeling and explanation from the heyday of rational empiricism to the rise of existentialism, or from the adventures of Candide to the metamorphosis of Gregor Samsa.

Like views on child-rearing, interpretations of the Enlightenment tend to vacillate between two poles; the one confronts us with the "heavenly city" of Kant's categorical imperative, Newton's laws, and Rousseau's religion of virtue, while the other dwells on his *Confessions* and primitivism, Johnson's pessimism, Kant's regulative ideas, and the passions released by the French Revolution. Which was the reality and which the façade? Whatever the answer to this question may turn out to be, any one-dimensional philosophy of the Enlightenment as intellectualist or anti-intellectualist can no longer be maintained.

The relativity of taste, morals, and even religion was already commonplace among the educated. To be sure, the relativity of truth still lay concealed, but surely this extension of the concept occurred to not a few, at least in its implicitness. In vain do we seek discord in the formal gardens of Versailles or the faith of deists, but Voltaire's *Candide* refutes more than "the pre-established harmony," and Pierre Bayle's celebrated skepticism could also touch the polemic of the *philosophes* themselves. No philosophical system comparable to the achievements of Leibniz, Spinoza, and Descartes was evolved in the eighteenth century, and the fragmentariness of the sciences, which became a standard complaint in the nineteenth century, could already be clearly discerned. The excitement touched off by the Lisbon earthquake hardly attests to a unified world view. Rousseau's distrust of the arts and sciences as ameliorative, Kant's notion of "radical evil" in human nature, the dehumanizing idealism of a Robespierre dispensing justice, the spirit of criticism becoming conscious of itself between the Scylla of dogmatism and the Charybdis of nihilism, the hedonism and sentimentality embodied in the best society of the day, and the religious revivals in England, Germany, and the United States— these manifestations should neither be dismissed as aberrations nor blown up out of proportion as a separate tradition. The ruptures and divisions in modern consciousness which often continue to be associated with nineteenth-century Romanticism were just as characteristic of the eighteenth century, although differently expressed. Romanticism and Enlightenment must be seen together not merely as negations of each other, nor as dialectical opposites, nor as cause and effect in time, but, metaphorically speaking, as ego and alter ego in the same personality classically defined by Pascal. As the Romantic composers adored Gluck's operas, Voltaire, Hume, Kant, and Rousseau (the great enlighteners) directly contributed to the emergence of "feeling" as a genuine alternative to explanation. It would appear then that modern subjectivity and objectivity were reciprocal from the outset of their development in the seventeenth century, and that the neglect of either in any major thinker resembles a Freudian slip rather than a possible exclusion.

Nature and History

Haydn's *Creation* is a musical equivalent of deist edification. Enchanting melody and pictorial phrases coalesce into a harmonious pattern marred by no more than a brief storm, a bit of natural evil to set off the over-all good. What a different world from Bach's tense dialogue between God and man or Mozart's sudden plunges into darkness amidst light-heartedness and joy! Original sin is absent from Haydn's *Creation*, and since man is in no need of redemption, all is bathed in childlike innocence. Haydn of course did write in another style, but this particular score, presumably delineating the origins of human history, remains a symbolic milestone of eighteenth-century aspirations. Bach is the Christian theist wrestling with the dualism of sin and grace, his powerful fugues conveying the unity of irreconcilables and his chorales the inexhaustible mercy of God. In Mozart's operas the struggle has been secularized, but without any lessening of tension. Reconciliation and forgiveness can come only after much misunderstanding and suffering. His most cheerful ideas are rarely out of reach of the sinister *Urgrund* below. But Haydn, on the whole, is reassuring and relaxing. His humor never fails him.

These three musical giants of the eighteenth century were masters of disciplined inspiration. Yet the differences between them are more crucial than the often insensitive knowledge of musicologists would allow. Of the three, Haydn, it would be generally agreed, is most typical of his age. And also the most limited. There is something missing from the horizons of his *Creation* which analogously is covered up in Holbach's understanding of man, or Hume's of experience, or Voltaire's of religion. Being a part of reality it is of course always present, but so great was the passion for order in the Enlightenment that the contingent was apt to be banished, trivialized, or removed to a neutral corner. Haydn's *Creation* nevertheless is a wonderful work to hear in its evocation of dawn before shadows fell on human existence. Likewise the writings of the *philosophes* have a charming freshness of their own, though their total effect is disappointing.

The quest for order is evident in all man does. It may well be the root of civilization. Western philosophy and science stand out by virtue of their methodological rigor for discovering orderly processes in nature. Philosophy from its very beginnings saw the world as a cosmos. Already the contribution of the Ionian thinkers in this direction proved momentous. Christianity also, particularly in its emphasis on tradition and theological structure, abetted the drive for grasping things whole. It was, however, only with the rise of modern science, its mechanical modes of explanation and mathematical language of notation, that the quest for order fell into idolatry.

Ionian speculation was religious as well as scientific, thus preserving in men's minds a sense of mystery about the universe. The rationalist Socrates had his daimon, who told him what not to do; Plato's thought in its highest moments modulates into myth; and Aristotle's concept of matter as mere potentiality serves as a foil to his otherwise cut-and-dried vision of reality. For the Stoics nature was suffused with life like an organism. So far as Greek mythology and tragedy are concerned, their roots in the irrational scarcely need reiteration. Precisely because we admire the Greek achievement for its moderation, control, balance, and Apollonian grace is it so important not to lose sight of its affinities with reality below and beyond explanation and rational synthesis. The Atomists, to be sure, tried to reduce reality to atoms in a void, but (quite apart from their limited success in this endeavor) they never developed an inclusive view of existence comparable, say, to Plato's, Homer's, or that of Sophocles. In any event, Greek civilization by and large took into account Dionysos next to Apollo, and in its supreme moments placated them both.

It was largely in reaction against scholastic rigidity that modern philosophy and science took wing. This fact is not altered by apologetic revisionists who now view the high Middle Ages as the harbinger of Renaissance wisdom. They never manage to explain why most major philosophers and scientists from the fourteenth century on had good reason for fearing the Church and placed themselves in ever more open opposition to scholasticism, authoritarianism, and enthusiasm. It is no complete denigration of the Middle Ages to see it full of devils, heretics, mysterious voices, ritualistic trappings, and dogmatic symbols of eternity. Rightly sinister as its inhibiting narrowness struck the pioneers of humanism and the new knowledge, still with all its blunders it did not cut off man from the contingent aspects of Being. The road to one's eternal end had been mapped once and for all, but the surprises in store for Dante in the *Purgatorio* remained, as it were, to the discretion of a force that could shake the foundations of earth and everything. In reacting against medieval spirituality and dogmatism modern philosophy and science embraced an unprecedented idolatry of order.

The Enlightenment inherited the already dehumanized universe of Descartes, Locke, Hobbes, and Newton. (Spinoza and Leibniz because of special religious motivation managed to preserve a modicum of life in their systems; Newton did so in his uninfluential writings.) This universe is "demythologized" of almost everything that makes human life worth living. The reality left to us consists of primary qualities, matter in motion, self-evident tautologies, and a pathological fear of being deceived. The deity, or rather the First Cause, becomes a helpful abstraction for tying together the loose ends. Poetry and the whole world of internal experience are consigned to something at best not far removed from illusion. The reality of the world to which men are sensitive all of the time is dismissed as trivial compared to the movements of the planets. Never before—but, alas, often since—had philosophy grown so divorced from human existential concerns. The split of science from the liberal arts which continues to be bemoaned in the twentieth century is no chimera. Contra Pascal and Leibniz it emerged in the seventeenth century to plague generations to come. The citadel of modern science, glorious and impressive as it appears in its own light, was purchased dearly at the price of creeping individual and collective materialism, reflecting in turn the sacrifice of man's *Lebenswelt* to the pseudo sciences and to caprice.

It can be argued on the other side that the Enlightenment consolidated the scientific breakthroughs of the great seventeenth-century thinkers by applying their method to the problems of society. Did not the Encyclopedists pave the way for the French Revolution by initiating multiple reforms, laying the foundations for modern penology, education, toleration, and good table manners? Did not the brilliant talk of serious matters in the drawing rooms of Paris become a model for all but Dostoevsky's characters to emulate in their pursuit of truth? These matters are true enough in a general way, nor should they be deemed without merit. But the Enlightenment, for all its humanism and liberal zeal, could never adequately transcend its seventeenth-century legacy—a universe divided into what can be known with certainty and the rest, which can be sensed only with trepidation and suspicion of prejudice. Perhaps this accounts in part for how naïvely Rousseau thought of natural man, Voltaire of Jesus at Gethsemane, Robespierre of virtue in the State, and Hume of getting rid of myth. Even in penetrating their climate of opinion, they were deceived by "nature's" incongruence with human realties. Indeed, to cope with man in history (both in theory and practice) requires tools other than common sense.

History presents us with a world full of confusion and conflict which, from the time of Aristotle, philosophers, theologians, and then scientists have been prone to ignore or deprive of true import. In this, however, they did not succeed, and possibly there is a hint of poetic justice in the suggestion that since the eighteenth century these daemonic forces have come to haunt them. Not that historians like scientists ever cease looking for over-all patterns of development and meaning, but if they are good historians they will deal just as scrupulously with the bizarre, the unexpected, the seemingly senseless, and the accidents and betrayals. Even Hegel, who would have liked to transform human history into dialectical movement, could not help but admit the "ruse of reason" into his system. History attests the precariousness of human action and the mysterious place of time-events in nature. While Hume, Voltaire, and Gibbon figure as pioneers in the "scientific" writing of history, it can hardly be claimed that they ever understood the distinguishing characteristics of their craft. Save for one of these—the daemonic—it is impossible here to review the now commonplace differentiation between the realm of repetitive predictable processes and the area of unique, freely chosen acts. In fact, the "daemonic" can be singled out as the alter ego of Lockean reasonableness crying out for recognition. It was not the genius of Newton, but that of Herder and the German Romantics which inspired the new history.

Some music lovers will not listen to the Passions of Bach because, they feel, it is a travesty of the horrible events narrated in the Gospels to invest them with breathtakingly beautiful sound. And no doubt they have a genuine insight into the daemonic. For the supreme artists the depths and heights of human experience invariably make transcendent contact.

In his remarkable autobiography Mark Rutherford illustrates three major manifestations of the daemonic. First, as the distortion of a quality or act into its opposite:

> It may be asked, How are we to distinguish heavenly instigation from hellish temptation? I say, that neither you nor I, sitting here, can tell how to do it. We can lay down no law by which infallibly to recognize the messenger from God. . . .[1]

Secondly, as the deliberately pursued divorce of feeling and reason:

> "What is the matter?"
> "You must know. You must know that ever since we have been married you have never cared for one single thing I have done or said, that is to say, you have never cared for me. It is *not* being married."
> It was an explosive outburst, sudden and almost incoherent, and I cried as if my heart would break.
> "What is the meaning of all this? You must be unwell. Will you not have a glass of wine?"
> I could not regain myself for some minutes, during which he sat perfectly still, without speaking, and without touching me. His coldness nerved me again, congealing all my emotion into a set resolve, and I said—
> "I want no wine. I am not unwell. I do not wish to have a scene. I will not, by useless words, embitter myself against you, or you against me. You know you do not love me. I know I do not love you. It is all a bitter, cursed mistake, and the sooner we say so and rectify it the better."

The colour left his face; his lips quivered, and he looked as if he would have killed me.

"What monstrous thing is this? What do you mean by your tomfooleries?"

I did not speak. . . .[2]

Third, as paradoxical appearance:

I was confounded. Who could have dreamed that such tragic depths lay behind that serene face, and that her orderly precision was like the grass and flowers upon volcanic soil with Vesuvian fires slumbering below? I had been altogether at fault, and I was taught, what I have since been taught over and over again, that unknown abysses, into which the sun never shines, lie covered with commonplace in men and women, and are revealed only by the rarest opportunity.[3]

A fourth form is idolatry—the state of being infinitely concerned about a finite matter. At this point it may not be amiss to enumerate a number of instances of the daemonic as here defined.

What immediately comes to mind is Luther's predicament and that of other devout Christians who at times could not be sure of distinguishing the voice of God from Satan's. On a less exalted plane, it often happens that an act carried out in the best of faith brings results diametrically opposed to those intended. Hitler doubtless worked to create a thousand-year Reich; he died leaving Germany a shambles. Many a couple get married sincerely persuaded of needing each other only to induce mutually unbearable hell. In these examples of daemonic distortion the intentions of those involved may be perfectly forthright, so far as they understand themselves. What brings about the unexpected turn of events is the unpredictability of circumstances or, in St. Paul's famous phrase, the fact that all of us here on earth see through a glass darkly. How many things are resplendent without and rotten within! The philosopher who comes along *after a while* to remind us that sense perception is deceptive never shows up at the moment when we must actually choose.

The situation is somewhat different in Dostoevsky's classic legend of Christ's betrayal in *The Brothers Karamazov*. All Christianity in the world is perforce nominal Christianity. The theme of Christ being crucified again by His own Church constitutes the ultimate absurdity inherent in this paradox. What heightens the effect is that all is done with deliberation. Organized religion like everything else has its legitimate claims which must be defended. The Grand Inquisitor makes people repent just as Cipolla in Thomas Mann's "Mario and the Magician" makes them dance—after he has brandished his whip and hypnotized their wills.

A second significant expression of the daemonic is idolatry. Husbands who seemingly enjoy being browbeaten by their wives fall familiarly into this category. It is extremely difficult to delimit genuine emotion from possessive excitement, especially since the two intermingle in even the purest affection. Nevertheless, those who love and those who idolize each other stand out pretty sharply. What is daemonic about idolatry of this sort is the self-destruction of the person presumably fulfilling himself through a particular attachment to someone else. Heathcliffe in *Wuthering Heights* exercises such fascination on all who meet him that not a few are drawn to their downfall. And he certainly cannot be described as lovable.

Where in the past two centuries daemonic idolatry has become most prevalent is in politics. Socialism, communism, nationalism, fascism—each and every one of these was a "path to utopia." In eliciting from millions a veneration incommensurate with its possibilities it gave rise to an idolatry of political action whose fateful consequences still hang in the balance. The cult of Hitler in Nazi Germany, of the Party among left-wing intellectuals, of the masses in socialist thinking, of good intentions in liberalism, and well-known related phenomena, are evidence enough of an idolatry partly induced by the breakdown of traditional religion, partly the outcome of the traumatic impact of industrialism on humanist dreams. Again and again since the French Revolution have reigns of terror been instituted for the benefit of humanity: the very spokesmen for a new social justice without a discernible twitch of conscience perpetrate crimes that make past tyrannies look angelic. The nonbarbaric terror (of the mind rather than the glands) that has become such an integral feature of modern history is immortalized in Goya's etchings from *The Caprices*, "The Dream of Reason Produces Monsters" and "Experiments." Rousseau, who at one stage did see through the illusion of automatic progress, also helped perpetuate ideological fanaticism.

A third form of the daemonic is exemplified by the divorce of feeling from reason already celebrated, so to speak, in Laclos's *Les Liaisons dangereuses,* let alone the weeping spells of the author of "The Profession of Faith of the Savoyard Vicar." Some speak of it as the abstraction of lust from love; others, seeing more deeply, recognize it as a state of passionlessness where the individual excites himself heteronomously in order to act at all. (Twentieth-century dictators are often praised for their dedication.) In this post-Freudian era it is not really surprising that an excessively rationalistic culture like the Enlightenment would attempt to come to terms with the inner life, surreptitiously. The "hero" of Laclos's novel calculates his conquests with scientific rigor. As someone remarked in another connection, he has plenty of method but no character. A typical modern condition! Even in the process of love-making his scheming continues, as on one memorable occasion he appears to be taking notes on the nude back of his beloved. His total uninvolvement as a person in any of his affairs is truly daemonic and anticipates that other great document on modern sensibility— Kierkegaard's *Diary of the Seducer.*

Nor can Laclos's fictional character be taken as an isolated instance. The libertinism and callousness of the French bourgeoisie in the latter half of the eighteenth century contrasts decidedly with the atmosphere of the *salon* and the sober hymns to virtue *philosophes* composed and disseminated. It is a speculative question whether Kant's virtual exclusion of natural desire from moral status did not have some origin in the debased emotional life of eighteenth-century society. There is no doubt that Kant acknowledged a fundamental rift between the head and the heart, and finding the latter "radically evil" ("every man has his price") postulated absolute obligation above and beyond them both. Between the tears of Werther and the stratagems of Laclos's Valmont beckoned the Marquis de Sade to usher in a new phase in the breakdown of Christian humanism.

Nineteenth-century literature is filled with expressions of this daemonic rift between insensitive knowing and wayward feeling. There is the seminal figure of Goethe's Faust despairing of knowledge and succumbing, for a long while, to the tyranny of unsatisfied desire. And John Stuart Mill torn in two by the dictates of analysis and the appeal of poetry, although a recent British commentator came up with the illuminating idea that Mill was merely suffering from the strains of overwork. (The implication that British empiricists are subject to nervous breakdowns but not to spiritual crises is indeed a curious bit of Lockean psychologizing.) Stravrogin's "Confession" in Dostoevsky's *Possessed* is perhaps the "last" word on the subject. Stravrogin, knowing that in the closet in back of him a child is hanging itself, does not interfere, for he is reading his paper. Only this can explain such tales of our time as Kafka's "Penal Colony," Camus's *The Fall*, and Thomas Mann's *Doctor Faustus*.

The more general sense of "daemonic" as what startles or appears strangely paradoxical to us, being more immediately experienced, directs less attention to itself. In question here are sudden transitions of mood, spurts of power latent one moment and explicit the next, and striking incongruities both in life and art. It is the revelation of the human condition, in contrast to the neutrality of nature, with all its ambiguities and discords. Nature of course can be destructive, terrifying, and grotesque in evolving irregular instances of species, but having no will of its own it can never be daemonic. Historians and artists, quite rightly, have been designated as possessing special insight into the daemonic structures of existence. Still, the over-all task of the historian remains descriptive.

He tells us to the best of his knowledge what men have done, not evading the rough spots, and, on the other hand, not usually exploring them very deeply. The classical ancient and modern philosopher was uninterested in doing so because his methods prejudiced him to regard these matters as unreal or nonexplanatory.

But the artist or philosopher-artist has special insight into those aspects of reality which elude objectification and causal representation. Where ordinary language fails and symbolic logic is completely irrelevant his works confront us with unique cognition. To say that Bach's Passions or Mozart's *Don Giovanni* are daemonic is not to denigrate them, but to point out that they bring us face to face with truths that ordinarily would be too painful to bear. These glimpses into the hidden recesses of Being will always transcend a philosophy that sets out to reduce knowledge to explanation. Nor, surely, can passion or sensation be the answer. The artist divines something we have long suspected to be true without having the vision to see it. Suddenly we are confronted by it, overwhelmed, and whisper to ourselves: how in the world . . . he must be in league with the devil . . . he knows it all. This is daemonic! But, contrary to Rousseau, human existence is never simple. There is no "state of nature" to return to because there never was one to begin with. The human world is always as complex and precarious as human nature. And this nature has a history that nothing in nature at large resembles.

Dogmatism and Nihilism

The Enlightenment was as much the critic of reason as its apostle. Hume and Kant especially by questioning the foundations of traditional metaphysics became instrumental in opening the floodgates to the varieties of skepticism, relativism, and general anti-intellectualism. Moreover, the spirit of the *philosophes*, while reasonable and critical, was sooner or later destined to attack itself and produce the "free-floating intelligence" of the modern intellectual. In this process every starting point is questioned as being subject to further analysis. But analysis can never be a substitute for conviction, so that eventually the thinker finds himself in the position of an artisan with a set of tools which time and again he puts off using lest he make a mistake. What distinguishes philosophy since the Enlightenment from all its other phases is the degree of self-consciousness with which the philosopher embarks upon his perilous journey. He is conscious not so much of the objects of his understanding as of the understanding itself in the process of thinking. Here lie the roots of the critical spirit, which started out so hopefully eliminating dogma and ended up consuming itself.

When Socrates criticized the unlearned ignorance of his contemporaries he did this with definite standards in mind. His irony was directed against false and hollow knowledge, but he knew the direction and goal of authentic reflection. His task to perforate pretentiousness was predicated on the belief that true virtue and wisdom were attainable through dialectic. Had he not believed in the truth of the proposition that virtue is knowledge, it is doubtful whether his midwifery would have had any but a comic effect. The Socratic critique was so far-reaching precisely because it did not occur in a vacuum. Even on the supposition that Plato read a good deal of his own idealism into Socrates, there remains the person of Socrates—incorruptible in his quest for the good life.

As regards eighteenth-century criticism the situation is quite different. Voltaire, for example, was clearly opposed to religious fanaticism, superstition, metaphysical cant, and tyranny. But what exactly was he for? What should man do after all the hated abuses and authorities had been destroyed? The appeal to what all rational men would consent to at all times was itself being vitiated by the growth of historicism. The insight that rational beings in China did not consent to the same propositions and practices as rational beings in Paris was not confined to Montesquieu. Hence there developed an ever-increasing reliance on personal subjectivity and inner certainty. The *philosophes,* however, were not Christian enthusiasts: not only did they reject the Church, but also their passion for universal consent did not allow them to trust any inner voices in the determination of truth. For them Pascal's "reason of the heart" exemplified the principle of insufficient reason. Rational understanding could pierce illusions, but could it by itself establish a "science" of basic truths?

Enlightenment criticism encouraged a ceaseless chase for a quarry becoming more and more obscure; a type of Romantic utopianism, always living in the future and always being discontented with the past that had become the present. From now on things are right only insofar as they change. With each realized end another is immediately sought. How different this turned out from the Socratic injunction to know oneself and to live authentically in the present. Voltaire, like contemporary analytic philosophers, is chiefly remembered for what he did not like.

The lesson of the Enlightenment with regard to criticism is that it can clear the atmosphere, but it cannot create a new one unaided. Kant, having repudiated dogmatic metaphysics, posed but never satisfactorily answered the question whether "new" metaphysical truths are in fact possible. In affirming the indispensability of metaphysics for man he saw deeper than Hume, but within the framework of theoretical knowledge he could not find room for the expression of this instinct. If faith in anything that cannot be thus known is dogma, then nihilism would appear to be the only alternative. Kant, to be sure, anticipated James in arguing for the necessity of some belief beyond discursive analysis, yet his "regulative ideas" form an uneasy alliance with his commitment to *Aufklärung*. It was really only after the reaccommodation of subjectivity in the nineteenth century (Kierkegaard, Nietzsche) that the Humean-Kantian dilemma could be relieved.

Objectivity and Authenticity

William James can hardly be charged with Teutonic metaphysical mysticism, which makes it particularly interesting to observe how this lucid empiricist (steeped in Hume) came to embrace an idea akin to the Kierkegaardian *"leap."* If there is no science of values save in the negative sense of discarding those opposed to "free" inquiry, man must either resign himself to an inauthentic existence of nondecision (an impossibility in fact) or "leap" over and above the precepts of critical reason and empirical belief. James deserves great credit for extending the concept of experience in the existential direction of truth *for* in addition to truths *about* man. Hume and Kant had brilliantly delineated the limits of objectivity, but neglected to shift their focus from the realm of thought to the predicament of the thinking person. They were of course far too sophisticated to espouse anything like the dogmatic materialism against which James inveighed. Nevertheless, what they left unsaid encouraged the champions of "scientism" in the nineteenth century to dogmatize and tyrannize. Robespierre's religion of reason, short-lived during the Revolution, became a dogma as pernicious as any other. James challenged its authenticity for human beings by spelling out both its formal contradictions as well as its highly debatable consequences. In any case, scientific humanism, James was able to show, is no more cognitive a creed than Christian humanism or the presumed neutrality of agnostics. The question is not merely what man can know but how he decides to live.

Progress and Despair

Leibniz had maintained that there were no leaps in nature, but in the course of the eighteenth century it became increasingly evident that there were plenty of rifts—at any rate, between faith and reason, society and the individual, thought and existence, necessity and contingency, and not least in men's souls. While Christian dualism declined, new varieties came to the fore, and Leibniz's vision of a "great chain of being" harmoniously accommodating science, religious belief, freedom, and the logic of good and evil gradually collapsed, splintering into atomic but hardly self-sufficient units. On the one hand, the resulting autonomy for the arts and sciences accelerated their development and indeed led to some

remarkable achievements; on the other, there set in an
irreparable loss of a sense of wholeness and a tendency on
the part of each autonomous unit to make itself the
supreme arbiter. Within a century the proud and isolated
monads of Leibniz were (in their human manifestation)
becoming more and more often the lonely and anxious
individuals of Romanticism; yet, ironically enough, it was
only now that the idea of progress flourished as a gospel.
It is rather doubtful whether Leibniz would have felt
comfortable in the Crystal Palace.

The idea of progress rested on a partial truth: the
undeniable advance in learning and particularly in science
since the seventeenth century. Moreover, the prognosis
that this progress would continue proved correct. Science
and industrialism have repeatedly revolutionized modern
life. Where Turgot, Condorcet, Helvetius, and Comte were
led astray was in their evaluation of these developments.
They simply failed to see them as but one factor in a whole
way of life. It is easy enough to recite the blessings of
technology, and its drawbacks are analogously obvious.
The heart of the matter is linking both to the total life
of the individual and the community of which he is a
part. And in this the apostles of progress failed miser-
ably. Often seduced by the crudest mechanistic and
environmental thinking, they lost sight of the inner life of
man, which cannot be satisfied by science alone. Just as
tourists do not necessarily feel well in the best-run hotel,
it was silly to suppose, even under conditions of ideal
realization, that human happiness is proportionate to the
degree of science in society. Weren't things getting better
all the time? Wasn't medieval superstition yielding unerringly to cogent argument and enlightenment? Hadn't mankind done with the Dark Ages? The poets, of course, would
not understand because they were too sensitive.

Amidst the wreckage and despair of the twentieth
century the charge of hindsight is readily leveled against
the contemporary critic of progress. It will also be suggested, with incredible naïvete, that science really hasn't
had a chance yet, for we must wait till man be morally
worthy of its great promise. Surely this was always the

point at issue. Will a scientific civilization adequately prepare man to live happily not only in and with it, but with himself? The champions of progress as well as the German humanist aesthetes assumed that *Entwicklung* lies in the acquisition of knowledge, taste, and experience. In short, to know more is to become more autonomous and human. The typical hero in nineteenth-century fiction realizes himself by becoming shrewd, well to do, and famous. Why, asks Dostoevsky in *Letters from the Under-world*, is this necessarily so? And, consistent with a negative answer to this question, he proceeds to write *Entwicklungsromane* in which the hero develops from a condition of intellectual pride to one of Christian charity. Dostoevsky's theme is the despair of the mind that has conquered all but its relationship to itself. Our trouble today is not that we haven't morally caught up with science, but that the religion of science makes it harder and harder for us to catch up with ourselves.

One is free of course to disagree with Dostoevsky's answer, but the very fact that there is another possibility of human fulfillment besides individual and collective materialism damns the idea of progress as generally held in the nineteenth century. For the validity of this idea presupposed an absolute commitment to the direction of Western civilization as it emerged in the late seventeenth and throughout the eighteenth century. Not only was this taking an exceedingly narrow view of Western civilization, but by 1800 the weaknesses even within that particular version of it were already so glaring that it is hard to see how it could continue to serve for so long as a model. In any event, whatever ideal of self-realization is dominant for a particular age, there will always be individuals who see their salvation in deviating from it and seeking heaven somewhere else. How else could we account for world-liness in the Middle Ages, piety in the Enlightenment, and hope in the twentieth century? Certain it is that prog-ress in the modern world has left a huge void, and that next to its familiar advantages it has been responsible for unprecedented vulgarity, uprootedness, and self-alienation. Dostoevsky and Kierkegaard cannot be accused of hindsight in independently formulating this diagnosis over a hundred years ago.

Idealism and Dehumanization

Undoubtedly the least ambiguously felt Enlightenment ideal of all was "virtue." Believers, freethinkers, radicals, and atheists all joined in a chorus of praise and reverence for its cultivation and attainment. Rousseau wept contemplating its beauty, Voltaire contrasted it enthusiastically with the evils of revealed religion, and Kant identified it with the starry heavens above as being of supreme worth. Robespierre went so far as to suggest worship of it, and the British moralists saw it as the sixth infallible sense through whose universal approbation human welfare would be secured. Never does it appear to have occurred to any of these thinkers that crimes committed in the name of morality and law are most distinctly human, that the beast while ferocious and lacking in self-control, so to speak, is incapable of hypocrisy and studied cruelty. The French Revolution, ironically enough the culminating historical event of the eighteenth century, experienced the corruption of virtue into an ideological fanaticism devoid of all charity. This was but the first in a series of high-minded reigns of terror. In an age of licentiousness such as the latter half of the eighteenth century it is perhaps understandable that the "tyranny of virtue" should go unrecognized, just as the "tyranny of the majority" became a live idea when the "age of the masses" was already upon us. Only William Blake, who scarcely liked anything favored by his contemporaries, railed against the sterile claims of obligation as another instance of hated non-spontaneity. Even Wordsworth, Romanticism and all, wrote an "Ode to Duty."

The hold of virtue on the imagination of the eighteenth century can in large measure be accounted for by the ill repute of organized Christianity. Where (particularly with the two previous centuries in mind) society was seen as divided by religious wars and controversies, the moral sense with its "universal" injunctions stood out all the more resplendent. It was not till the nineteenth century that the relativity of morals became a serious problem. It was generally assumed that moral reverence cuts across all parochial borders in leading humanity to greater kindliness and decency. Inasmuch as knowledge was confined to universals, the Enlightenment quite logically linked virtue with truth. In a dedaemonicized world moral virtue appears like the grace of God.

But, as is well known, this was not the whole story. Virtue as part of the religion of reason had to be conjoined with happiness, if not in the present life then in the future. Kant also had to come to terms with eighteenth-century eudaemonism. It has always been evident that there is no reliable moral justice on earth. This is offensive to the understanding. Sooner or later we must be assured that the virtuous will get their reward and the wicked their punishment. Thus Christianity slipped in the back door again. Hell for the sinner and paradise for the repenting in the eighteenth century becomes happiness for the virtuous and misery for the ill-behaved. The contrived ending of eighteenth-century novels is a classical expression of this faith. Prostitutes and highwaymen come to a bad end; English gentlemen and virgins can expect to live happily ever after.

No one will deny the significance of the moral in human experience. Yet noble as Kant's categorical imperative must strike us, it is still far from the mark of actuality. Kant is right in his insistence on the "good will" as the only unconditioned good, but in limiting its exemplifications to universally acceptable action he falls into a narrow moralism. Contrary to his asseverations, it happens that individuals who *under certain circumstances* lie, steal, break promises, or even treat a fellow human being merely as a means have a purer will than those who rigidly stick to principles. What saints often have in common with sinners is not defined by the categorical imperative. Self-sacrifice may go hand in hand with an exceptional line of conduct. Here the unusual act is committed not for the sake of selfish gratification but in the true interests of another. Self-righteousness and the path of virtue can be dangerously allied. Kant was also mistaken on another score. The greatest enemy of morality is not passion but insensitivity, not licentiousness but self-deception.

In *The Portrait of Zélide* Geoffrey Scott gives us a wonderful insight not only into the temperament of Mme de Charrière and her lover, Benjamin Constant, but also into the whole eighteenth century. Scott might just as well be weighing its ambiguities when he writes of their relationship:

> What is clear, and the sequel will show it still more clearly, is that this man and this woman, widely separated in age, obsessed each other. The attraction was between two minds, bewilderingly akin. To each the self-conscious analysis of every pulse and instant of life, of every problem and situation, was as necessary as a vice. Benjamin was a libertine when the mood was on him, just as in other moods he became an ambitious author or a politician; but he was a thinker always; and his intellect never worked with more startling clearness than when his emotions were involved. . . .
>
> On Madame de Charrière's side the obsession was natural enough. . . . She found in Benjamin a blend of fantasy and logic like her own, a creature as solitary as herself and as eagerly curious for every experiment in the human chemistry, craving, as she craved, insatiably, for a shared analysis of life. . . . By her quick understanding of him she had made herself the one fixed firm point in the *tour de force* of his life. She knew him—unpredictable, yet instinctively and almost childishly loyal; sophisticated, and yet wholly impulsive; frivolous, only to hide how deeply his seriousness was always baffled and perplexed. He might wear mask upon mask: she would not quarrel with it: she knew that the mask was as essential to him as what lay behind; neither more nor less. No other woman had done that. No other woman would have the brains to do it. Her hold on him was so great that she over-reached herself. She analyzed. She explored. She guided. One thing she did not understand in time: that Benjamin might weary of being understood.[4]

CHAPTER I

The Breakdown of Universal Order: Mozart and the Daemonic

The unheard-of success of *Don Giovanni* consists precisely in the variety of styles and yet the swelling of the styles into each other. Opera "buffa-seria," "dramma giocoso"—it becomes impossible to distinguish the nature of the *tone*. This seems to me to mark the presence of the demonic in Mozart.

Pierre-Jean Jouve[1]

In an extensive footnote to his *Dogmatik* Karl Barth pays this tribute to the genius of Mozart:

Why and in what sense can this man be called unique? Why has he, for him who can understand him, almost with every measure that passed through his mind and that he wrote down on paper, created music for which "beautiful" is an inadequate expression; music that for the "just" is not entertainment, nor pleasure, nor edification, but flesh and blood; music full of consolation and admonition, as they need it, never reduced to mere technique and never sentimental, but music "moving," free, and liberating, because wise, virile, and sovereign? Why can one maintain that he has a place in theology (especially in eschatology and cosmology) although he was no church father and not even a particularly devout Christian—and beyond that Catholic!—and, when not busy composing, according to our notions leading a somewhat fickle life. . . . He has heard the harmony of creation as providence in coherent form of which darkness is also a part, but in which darkness is not eclipse, also the deficiency which is no flaw, the sadness that cannot lead to despair, also the gloomy that is not transformed into the tragic, the infinite sorrow that nevertheless remains unconstrained to posit itself absolutely—precisely therefore also joyousness, but also its limits, the light that is so radiant precisely because it breaks through the shadows, sweetness that is also pungent and therefore does not carry satiety in its wake, life that is not afraid of death but knows it well. . . . In the music of Mozart—I ask whether one also finds this in any of his successors—we are dealing with an illuminating, I should like to say with a compelling proof that it is a slander of creation to ascribe participation in chaos to her because she includes a Yes and a No within herself, because one side of her is turned toward Nothingness and the other toward God. Mozart makes audible that creation praises the Lord also in its negative aspect and thus in its totality. . . .[2]

He returns to the subject in his *"Wolfgang Amadeus Mozart 1756/1956,"* [3] where, his admiration far from diminished, he makes too much of Mozart's ignorance of nonmusical culture. Although certainly Mozart was not an academic, his familiarity with languages and the major cultural currents of his day is incontestable. An ignoramus would hardly have set to music *The Marriage of Figaro,* Beaumarchais' comedy which is often thought to have anticipated the social upheavals of the French Revolution. Moreover, Barth the theologian is on dubious grounds in singling out for praise Mozart's liturgical music. No doubt there are wonderful moments in these works, particularly in the *Requiem,* but, taken as a whole, they do not measure up to the incandescence of the operas, piano concertos, chamber music, and symphonic music. This does not mean that Mozart's music is irreligious, but as the religiousness of modern man generally, its deepest expressions occur outside the Church. Unlike Bach's, Mozart's imagination was fired not so much by the Word of God as by the words of men. No one will dispute Barth's ignorance of the music sung in heaven, but if the angels have any resemblance to men, they should be credited with enough sense to program Bach's cantatas together with Mozart's "secular" works for their angelic concerts without fear of succumbing to worldliness.

Barth here is reacting against the father of modern dialectical theology, who with deeper insight but also with his love for paradoxical exaggeration had identified Mozart's music with the aesthetic stage on life's way.[4] Art of course can become an idol destructive of man's ethical-religious responsibilities, but it can also serve to reveal the depths of our existence. Kierkegaard, it must be admitted, failed sufficiently to distinguish the diverse potentialities inherent even in the daemonic. Yet it is unnecessary to share his evaluations of his own categories in order to learn from him. If he is wrong in suggesting that man has to choose between Mozart and Christ, Barth makes a worse mistake in evading the problematical situation out of which Kierkegaard's harsh judgment evolved. The fact remains that no one has written more profoundly on Mozart so as to make it impossible to disagree without initially being indebted.

The central theme in *Don Giovanni* is the intermingling of freedom and dread. Giovanni glides through the world like a god, radiating irresistible charm and suffused with seemingly inexhaustible energy. His main objective in life is the seduction of desirable women, but he pursues it with such devotion and uninhibited feeling that self-indulgence appears invested with beauty. His unwillingness to sleep or rest is daemonic, as is his indefatigable loyalty to the sensual principle. God created man in his own image. This means that even though creatures, we are to some extent endowed with divine energy. Don Giovanni has chosen to utilize this precious gift for the fulfillment of his sensual pride rather than for "the perfection of his nature." In this connection it must be noted that, unlike his heirs, he is not an especially calculating or despairing lover. He does not dream of the unattainable and then discard it on having found it. Nor does he show any particular interest in experimenting with women in order to gain greater self-knowledge. Nor, as far as the libretto of the opera is concerned, is he a crass pragmatist solely motivated by the recurring taste of success. There is an ironic contrast between his thousand and three conquests in Spain alone and the absence of a single triumph in the whole course of events Mozart set to music. Mozart's hero-villain is still something of a preface to the age of frustration and aberration he helped to make famous.[5] All he desires is the immediacy of satisfaction heightened by a fast turnover. His single-minded application to the preservation and regeneration of a single value could under other circumstances easily be mistaken for religious martyrdom. If man could think of God as consistently and patiently as Don Giovanni thinks of womanhood he would indeed be saved. Giovanni is a fine illustration of a basic theological insight: man is free to destroy his own freedom. This possibility points to the threat of the daemonic in human existence.

But man is also in dread. By what stroke of genius does Mozart towards the end of the Catalogue aria introduce the bassoons with a sharply rhythmic, unexpectedly brooding and ominous phrase to remind us that all is not purely laughable even in a comic situation! At this point in the opera the accented bass figuration is but a shadow of darkness briefly beclouding the prominent light into which Leporello casts his master. With the progress of the action it assumes spiritual significance. Leporello relishes the master-slave relationship thrust upon him. For survival he is at the mercy of Don Giovanni's pleasure, but he prefers this state of affairs to any alternative position in life requiring a greater degree of responsibility. In spite of his intermittent threats to break with his master, he bathes contentedly in the dazzling sunshine of Giovanni's glory until and unless danger to his life becomes imminent. He pretends to be entirely conversant with Giovanni's career, though it is clear from the start that he lacks not only his master's animal magnetism, but his faith and recklessness as well. Again and again, where Don Giovanni is prepared for decisive action Leporello pines to cower in a corner hoping against hope that the association that enables him to shine will not be held against him once its radiance is eclipsed. Where

Giovanni successfully reduplicates intention in action, however frustrating its consequences may turn out to be, Leporello can only be himself as his sidekick.

His dread, of course, is patently human, and therefore intelligible. Like most of us he finds evil more enticing than good, especially when another is held to account for so ingeniously manipulating it. But he has a conscience that troubles him at times and a fear of physical annihilation which throttles any total involvement in the irregular, however scintillating to the curiosity. Where Giovanni represents the sensual superman aloof from freedom's attendant restraints, Leporello is his dialectical opposite, a willing slave to convention trembling to preserve his necessary bondage. In *Sickness unto Death* Kierkegaard contrasts these two types of despair: the *despair of infinitude as being due to the lack of finitude* and the *despair of finitude as being due to the lack of infinitude.* Giovanni's will is "fantastic," "limitless," virtually unrelated to his general humanity. He is capable of creating hell on earth because the world means nothing to him beyond being a source of unending pleasure. The fanaticism of a religious mystic who professes to despise mere finitude in order to please God has a good deal in common with this nonmorality, which respects no personal obligations, immunizes itself to vicarious suffering, and acts according to the maxim that concrete particulars matter little. "Generally the fantastical," writes Kierkegaard, "is that which so carries a man out into the infinite that it merely carries him away from himself and therewith prevents him from returning to himself." Leporello, on the other hand, is unaware of his true condition:

> While one sort of despair plunges widely into the infinite and loses itself, a second sort permits itself as it were to be defrauded by "the other." By seeing the multitude of men about it, by getting engrossed in all sorts of worldly affairs, by becoming naive about how things go in this world, such a man forgets himself . . . does not dare to believe in himself, finds it too venturesome a thing to be himself, far easier and safer to be like others, to become an imitation, a

number, a cipher in the crowd. . . . What is called worldliness is made up of just such men, who (if one may use the expression) pawn themselves to the world.[6]

Mozart spiritualizes this drama through music that can only be described as heavenly. The principal characters as a rule sing melodies transfiguring even their negative moods into transparent loveliness, though not without occasional suggestions of the despair lurking beneath superficially healthy-looking, robust, and cheerful countenances. The masterly score reflects the interplay of external sparkle and inner uneasiness throughout the opera. Of special interest in this respect is the trio following the death of Donna Anna's father. Suddenly the tremendous excitement generated by Giovanni's nocturnal intrusion dies down as the participants join in the kind of song which can pierce the soul. It is a genuine sublimation of *Zerrissenheit.* Then there is the pointed change of mood from *"Fin ch'han dal vino"* to the masked trio wherein the victims soberly pledge themselves to joint revenge before accepting Giovanni's bold invitation to his ball. And the ball itself! Where else in art or literature can one find an analogous suggestion of the licentiousness and formalism so uneasily interfused in Enlightenment life? To the strains of conflicting dances played by different orchestral groups on and off stage Mozart allows tremendous tension to build up. For a moment we are disarmed by the brilliance of the setting—lights, velvet, shining metal and glass, the graciousness of Giovanni as host. We are almost persuaded by his intrinsic goodness—if only it were permitted lasting expression in congenial surroundings such as these—when Zerlina's scream breaks the spell. The dancers are interrupted. Mozart's music at once plunges us into the ensuing turmoil. It is as if on the spur of the moment we turned from Rousseau's *Social Contract* to a chapter in his *Confessions* or from Kant's *Introduction to the Metaphysics of Morals* to his discussion of radical evil in *Religion within the Bounds of Reason.*

Don Giovanni remains unrepentant, insolent, and impervious to change, even when confronted by the Statue of the Commendatore. It is sensualism militant and resentful of interference which informs his whole bearing in the face of impending disaster. As if nothing were amiss he sits down to a table worthy of the highest humanistic refinement Europe had cultivated since the Renaissance. So revealing is the contrast between his imperviousness and the sprightly melodies played by onstage musicians to enhance the conviviality of the setting that, especially to the modern listener, it conveys a Dostoevskian insight into God-repudiating defiance posing as pious equanimity. There is no question about Giovanni's having the best of times. He goes so far as brazenly to invite his judge to share it with him. Where so many contemporary composers choose to represent the horribly fascinating through violent dissonance signifying nothing, Mozart, a wiser psychologist to say the least, envelops Giovanni's presumptuous indifference in merry reminiscences from *Figaro* and snatches from minor operas. His last supper becomes an occasion for infectious merry-making.

But the illusion of a humble place beyond moral good and evil at Giovanni's table proves quite ephemeral. Accompanied by running scales simple enough for children to practice, Giovanni makes a fiery entrance into hell. Reminiscent of Dante's great sinners in the *Inferno*, he does not despair of his personality even after the ghastly consequences of his way of life have been fully spelled out for him. Leporello still possesses enough of man's animal fear of the bizarre to desist from openly challenging the transcendent powers. Ethically he is less unrepentant than Giovanni, dialectically he lacks his religious irreligiousness to be damned by deliberate choice. Leporello's physical survival serves to underscore the Christian notion of charity for those too weak to help or hang themselves. Seeking a master more appreciative of his talents, he joins in the controversial final chorus celebrating the Enlightenment faith in requited virtue.

What kind of a comedy or tragedy is *Don Giovanni?* At one moment Mozart confronts us with the terror of underworld flames, at the next he pours forth gentle, directionless melody. What sense, if any, the listener asks himself in this connection, do human fortunes make? Instead of suggesting any unambiguous answer to that question Mozart lets the first violins play a final maddeningly quick theme—a detached commentary on the whole previous action. So long as we can view our follies with a suspension of emotion we need not despair of ourselves altogether. The very fact that the human race does not merely consist of Giovannis, Leporellos, Masettos, and Zerlinas, but also includes an occasional Mozart to sing about them is in itself a reaffirmation of human dignity and self-transcendence. What are the last strains of *Don Giovanni* but genius rejoicing in existence, however confused, however baffling? Because the world for Mozart never lost its fundamental goodness he was able to express the dialectic between light and darkness without courting fate.

The ending of *Don Giovanni* has been the subject of considerable speculation and controversy. A good deal of this rests first of all on a superficial acquaintance with Mozart's music in general, and, secondly, on the indiscriminate application of essentialist criteria for dramatic and emotional consummation to a profoundly concrete work of art.[7] Naturalism as well as romanticism in its undialectical forms insists on seeing a visible consistency in events which from a finite perspective they rarely disclose. Thus it is morally satisfying that a villain like Don Giovanni should become the victim of his own unbridledness, but to stress his undeniable charm in spite of his character distracts dangerously from his merited doom. Or, if Mozart had intended to conceive his theme comically, why does his music express numerous tragic overtones? So contiguous are the depths of human depravity and greatness that reason aims to keep them apart whereas passion blurs their respective particularity through fusion. The love-death in *Tristan und Isolde* and the triumph of freedom in *Fidelio* illustrate these possibilities on the highest level of artistic realization. There is nothing obscure or ambiguous about the forces of evil being overcome by the good in Beethoven's delineation of abstract justice; on the other hand, Wagner's lovers literally lose themselves in sheer subjectivity. Mozart successfully avoids both the hypostatization as well as the cancellation of opposites by allowing his situations to retain their existential confusion. As in real life the death of a great public enemy is attended by manifestations ranging from gratitude to morbid mirth, so the destruction of Giovanni releases mixed feelings of tranquil expectation and recollection.

If the composer of *Don Giovanni* and the author of the *Diary of the Seducer* had been able to meet it is interesting to speculate how they might have influenced each other. Both men, curiously enough, looked somewhat alike, were recognized as geniuses by a number of close acquaintances, and remained largely misunderstood, even by their admirers, until the twentieth century. Kierkegaard adored Mozart's music, but the apostle in him feared the voice of the poet, and so he felt constrained to criticize one of the great loves in his life. Reacting against the confounding of cultural with Christian values generally characteristic of the educated middle class in nineteenth-century Europe, Kierkegaard set out to re-establish the autonomy of God-centered inwardness. What he found so questionable in reflective intellectuality conceived as an end in itself, was the tacit acknowledgment of human self-sufficiency by all its enthusiasts. They were convinced that by virtue of being sensitive or talented every man might theoretically participate in the liberating effects of aesthetic experience, while by virtue of God's grace only those can attain salvation who choose to accept Him and have been chosen as acceptable by Him. If man could understand himself through cultural activity alone, Biblical revelation would be superfluous at best. But Kierkegaard's objections to the religion of humanism have a wider basis than his corrective approach to the meaning of the Cross. Being a romantic himself both by temperament and the "aesthetic humanism" he had absorbed so readily, Kierkegaard gained an uncanny insight into the rapture-let-down-boredom-melancholy cycle of just listening to music or indulging religiously in some other variety of "higher pleasure." With Schopenhauer and Baudelaire he was one of the first searching critics of self-realization dispensing with a superseding goal. Nobody else so perspicaciously analyzed man's infinite tolerance for despair precisely when the mind, having conquered the body, claims recognition of absolute sovereignty.[8] Furthermore, he clearly saw the paralyzing ethical implications of any ultimate human concern in terms of introspective enjoyment. Music is especially prone to beguile us into states of euphoria during which the least demand for concrete service becomes a disturbing burden. Indeed it is not only in bohemian circles that one encounters a striking lack of correlation between self-fulfillment and self-sacrifice.

While from Kierkegaard's understanding of the "offense" of the Cross[9] the ideational vagueness and amoral immediacy of musical experience as a substitute for concrete faith can readily be grasped, it is less clear why he singled out the music of Mozart to exemplify the aesthetic mode of existence. Perhaps it is just a coincidence that the spread of existentialist philosophy since the First World War has been accompanied by a great Mozart revival. Without having to stress his place of honor in the record catalogues or his popularity, superior to Wagner's, in present-day opera houses, few would disagree that next to Bach he has become the most esteemed of serious composers, certainly in the eyes of the intelligentsia. Is it too farfetched to imagine a connection between the instability and anxiety of thinking people today and their preference for the kind of music which reveals and partly overcomes these negative characteristics? Kierkegaard was so unerringly prophetic in his philosophical and theological preoccupations that his choice of Mozart, a highly admired but largely misunderstood composer in the nineteenth century, fits in with his overall critique of that age. It would have been odd for him to meditate, say, on the "Ode to Joy," or Schiller's *Aesthetic Education of Man,* inasmuch as their acceptance by his own generation made these texts, at any rate, already spiritually suspect. Conceivably it was the deceptive uncomplicatedness of Mozart's art, its lack of a message and extraordinary clarity, which helped to arouse Kierkegaard's interest.

Quite likely he sensed its peculiar religious appeal to those who have striven for dogmatic neutrality and (like himself) for uncompromising honesty. If not pointedly Christian, this music, negatively speaking, neither was inspired by nor perpetuates an alternate myth such as the teleological conception of nature among the romantic composers or overriding love of national tradition ranging from Wagner's remythologizing of Teutonic deities to Smetana's intoxication by Czech woodlands and meadows. Mozart, Mörike imagined, asked the blinds to be drawn on his way to Prague though the scenery outside was undoubtedly beautiful. He was never an apostle, not even for Freemasonry, which *The Magic Flute* completely transcends. The still aristocratic orientation of his life and work kept him immune from the "music-for-something-or-other" crusades that swept so many nineteenth-century composers off their feet and continue to play havoc with the creative process even now. Mozart's music, never flippant, gloomy, or pretentious, bears witness to an absence of illusions which makes it dialectically less irreligious, perhaps ethically more profoundly idolatrous, than the diluted piety of nationalist composers. No wonder that Kierkegaard's attitude towards the Salzburg *Wunderkind* was highly ambivalent: his feeling that in Mozart's music the aesthetic and the religious, the genius and the prophet, are almost indistinguishably one. For Kierkegaard this possibility was a temptation that he feared: had he not hoped to become a poet in his own right?

Only Bach, whose Christianity in opposition to Kierkegaard's is explicitly cultural, has been as successful in giving joint expression to love of human and divine through music. And it is worth while to ask how Kierkegaard would have approached his fellow Lutheran; for in him he encounters a kind of nonnominal Christian genius which he himself possessed without ever doing justice to it in his self-interpretation. Bach would seem to weaken Kierkegaard's case against Mozart by virtue of having written every kind of music without on that account feeling any great threat or contradiction to his faith. Why was Kierkegaard so uneasy about being a Christian humanist on the plane of Bach or Milton when ostensibly this is what he could have been and was by his gifts in spite of himself? Superficially it is true that Mozart's operas concern themselves with the interplay of natural feelings—everything gratuitous, ephemeral, moody, and uncertain appearing in unabashed prominence as if life consisted of a series of seductions and preparatory erotic gymnastics. In this connection Kierkegaard was more than justified in calling attention to the decadent aspects of unbridled aestheticism. But it is one thing to criticize the make-believe world of opera (as Plato has criticized the poetry of Homer); another to perceive the consequences of an exclusive preoccupation with beauty (witness Rimbaud, Stefan George, Oscar Wilde, and their circles, whom Kierkegaard was disillusioning seventy years in advance); and yet a third to evaluate justly the total impact of a Mozart opera. Even if one should have to grant (which one doesn't!) that Mozart's operatic music is devoid of ethical-religious moments, it does not follow that the behavior of Mozart's characters on the stage is to be taken as a reliable guide to the conduct of men and women on earth. To insist, as Kierkegaard did, on the existential reduplication of rational insights, is not to be committed to the proposition that art be didactic.

No doubt the eroticism of the natural man receives preferential treatment in *Entführung, Figaro, Don Giovanni, Così,* and *The Magic Flute.* Mozart was a master at representing the dodges, vagaries, concealments, and white lies of frail and mischievous human beings. But it would be patently false to credit him with the view that this is all there is to being an animal walking on two legs. The delineation of attraction and repulsion between the sexes, to use Kierkegaard's own phrase, is coming to terms with one of life's "crucial situations." How could the diarist of the seducer in *Either/Or* or the narrator of the Banquet in *Stages on Life's Way* take issue with the eroticism of, say, *Don Giovanni?* Was not Mozart in fact doing something quite similar in illuminating the depths of human degradation and worth through an analysis of passion? Is there not an element of "indirect communication" in the haughtiness of the Countess, the servility of Leporello, the rages of Osmin, and the cynicism of Don Alfonso?

It has been standard practice to condemn the libretto of *The Magic Flute* as an absurd hodgepodge that only the genius of Mozart saved from oblivion. But there is another way of looking at it, and in the light of the range of moods which Mozart's score encompasses, possibly a more plausible one. *The Magic Flute* is a daemonic tale: the Queen of the Night, at the beginning of the opera shown as wronged by Sarastro, who stole her daughter Pamina, turns out to be a monster leading the forces of darkness against virtue and light. Sarastro, the supposed tyrant, reveals himself a sage dedicated to the pursuit of righteousness and purity. In short, their actual roles in the drama constitute a complete reversal of initial appearances. This ambiguity is further heightened by the ravishing song of the Three Ladies who, judging by the music Mozart wrote for them, sound like angels. They are in league with their Queen and Monostatos to destroy the Temple. Notwithstanding the absurdity of events, these do in their own terms point to "the marriage of heaven and hell" which is so characteristic of human existence. No wonder that Mozart, whose music is almost always on the threshold of the mood opposite from the one receiving dominant expression, felt himself drawn to this uncanny atmosphere. Quite apart from his still controversial involvement in Freemasonry, the mystery enveloping the characters of the action could not help but appeal to his genius for representing discord. The conceptual framework of rationalism was hardly adequate to allow for some of the grotesque happenings in *The Magic Flute*.

Even the "nonsense" with which presumably Mozart had to work is not quite as nonsensical as often supposed. Papageno and Sarastro respectively symbolize hedonism and the "categorical imperative," the lives of inclination and duty that Kant struggled to keep apart in his dualism.

One resembles the "noble savage" of Rousseau, the other embodies the highest ideal of Enlightenment virtue. Tamino in the tradition of Parsifal and Kafka's heroes is a wanderer in semidarkness of his ultimate goal. And Pamina is, in Freudian terms, ambivalently tied to her evil-minded mother. It is a solemn chorale that upholds the central theme of the opera:

> Der, welcher wandert diese Strasse voll Beschwerden,
> Wird rein durch Feuer, Wasser, Luft und Erden;
> Wenn er des Todes Schrecken überwinden kann,
> Schwingt er sich aus der Erde himmelan.
> Erleuchtet wird er dann im Stande sein,
> Sich den Mysterien der Isis ganz zu weih'n.[10]

As in *Don Giovanni* Mozart here is concerned with a central issue—the horror of death which must be conquered. In the end, to be sure, light prevails over darkness, but on the road man is exposed to each in the most unpredictable fashion. Mozart's music mirrors sublimely the doubts and frustrations of the struggle, yet like the chorale at the conclusion of a Bach cantata he also sings of triumphant wisdom and compassion. The world is full of demons, but they do not necessarily have the last word though they are not without charm.

The merely aesthetic (if there is such a pure type) in *Don Giovanni* is but a preface to the aesthetic-religious or irreligious. Underlying the surface themes of the opera—intrigue, murder, and seduction—is Mozart's intense preoccupation with the dialectic between hubris and nemesis, grace and damnation, redemption and punitive suffering. It is hard to find a major ethical or religious issue that is not touched on in the course of the drama: Giovanni's unmerited length of life to inflict pain on the comparatively innocent, his seemingly successful defiance of providence, Zerlina's reckless affection oblivious of consequences, Leporello's bootlicking, Masetto's well-meaning but wellnigh destructive stupidity, and Donna Anna's hysterical righteousness are but a few examples. The reconciliation scene in *The Marriage of Figaro* is ethical in import, not to mention the letter duet, in which Susanna and the

Countess epitomize genuine communion between two members of their sex, or Barbarina's air, which inexplicably breaks off in the middle after intoning an unexpected excruciating air of sadness.

Idomeneo is based on the story of Jeptha from the Old Testament, which Kierkegaard cites in *Fear and Trembling* as an instance of tragic heroism second only to Abraham's faith "by virtue of the absurd." [11] Mozart's *Idomeneo* is miraculously free both from Gluck's leanings towards the mannered and the romantics' sentimental idealization of the past. As to *Così fan tutte*, it is, among other things, a profound study in irony which Kierkegaard in the *Concluding Unscientific Postscript* linked with the ethical mode of existence insofar as any distinction between pretense and reality presupposes transcendence of and detachment from immediacy. Finally, the Pasha music in Act One of the *Entführung* exposes the presumptuousness attending worldly power by literally laughing it out of existence; and when the would-be abductors are caught by Osmin after having misused all their elaborate preparations, Mozart, by dint of a few interpolated measures before the action continues, opens up a yawning abyss, the nothingness not only of disappointed lovers but potentially, ever threatening to envelop us, of mankind at large. [12]

Before these discontented times, in which so many have become predisposed to discern uneasiness and torment in each profound expression of art, Mozart was commonly regarded as a cheerful composer who, contrary to his own basic inclinations, gave vent to private sorrows in a few late works. According to this view the outstanding characteristics of Mozart's scores (on the whole) are complete mastery of sonata form, restraint, lightness of touch, brilliance, and, most important, geniality. Occasional clouds may dampen without dispelling the underlying gay, rhythmic pulse of his compositions. Children should practice them at an early age not only on account of their technical simplicity but because they will be spared a while longer the disillusionment and sadness implicit, let us say, in Beethoven, Schubert, and Brahms. Exposure to these masters, some would argue, in order to make an impression, requires a certain familiarity with the facts of frustration and satiety mercifully confined to adult experience. Thus Mozart is seen to have possessed a remarkable gift for evoking the moods of childhood without falling into sentimentality or condescension. He is the composer of eternal youth from whose genius emanates a flood of pretty sound—singable, harmonious, and full of good spirits. He is a favorite of the gods,[13] the same gods whom Hölderlin in *Hyperion* vainly strove to reaccommodate to the Western tradition about ten years after Mozart's death.

An opposing school of thought, which has gained strength in the twentieth century, maintains that Mozart's music is problematical and soul-searching from the early G-minor Symphony (K. 183) through the "Dissonant" Quartet (K. 465) of the middle period to the Clarinet Concerto (K. 622). The representatives of this viewpoint share with many existentialists a pronounced insensitivity toward the happier moods of mankind. Without necessarily going so far as to deny the affirmative quality of Mozart's works, they tend to interpret it as an incidental feature, a kind of relief from the composer's hidden preoccupation with the decline of Western civilization. "Indeed," they will tell you, "there is a Mozart for our children, but he did not mean to address us who know all the horrors of life." Meticulously they will divide the works into expressions of eighteenth-century gallantry, youthful experiments, bread-and-butter divertimento writing, and so on, until they have isolated the quintessence of the real Mozart who is to be found in approximately a hundred compositions each of which either has a minor key signature, anticipates Beethoven's last quartets, or plunges us into the depths of melancholy suggestive of Chopin. These listeners can hardly get over the fact that the "*Et incarnatus est*" of the C-minor Mass (K. 427) is so outspokenly exhilarating, trills within trills, ascribing this fault not merely to the demands of virtuoso performers, but to Mozart's weakened faith in the Christian scheme of redemption. Thus he is seen as a musical prophet of contemporary doom and gloom. He is the composer of Dionysian passion from whose genius emanates a flood of beautiful sound resigned, sorrowful, and filled with ill forebodings. He is the last aristocratic humanist in music who had gleaned the meaninglessness of it all but kept the secret locked in a few select compositions until Sir Thomas Beecham and the First World War provided the catalyst that released it to the present generation.

Contrary to these two schools of thought, the daemonic in Mozart's music[14] is the coexistence and mutual interplay of the joy of Hyperion dancing at the dawn of history and the anxiety of Kierkegaard, Amiel, and Jacobsen face to face with nothingness. No discursive mediation of these two elements is possible, yet Mozart's music, without destroying the authenticity of either, expresses joyful affirmation always on the edge of profound nihilism. Just because music is capable of saying more than words, of expressing the inarticulate double feelings of the inner life, Mozart succeeds in confronting us with a major paradox as a unified experience. Philosophers, historians, and poets since the seventeenth century have analyzed and bemoaned the split soul of Occidental man. Painters like Rembrandt, Goya, and Van Gogh have movingly depicted the visible effects of this schism on a man's face or in his apprehension of ordinary objects. Music alone, among the arts, and Mozart's music par excellence, can encompass at once (for the right listener!), as they go hand in hand, the most dreadful doubts and a persisting obligation to carry on in spite of them.

The thought of a circular square, a benevolent devil, or a loving hate is absurd. Our language stipulates that these are incompatible concepts even though, taking the last, we have such an experience without being able to put it into words. Mozart actually turns this kind of unintelligible conjunction into concrete recognizable musical events with a logic of their own. Like a mystic he penetrates the core of anomalies to a unity of opposites which, being musical, continues to be temporal. Composing towards the end of the eighteenth century between the "pre-established harmony" and the "age of anxiety," no longer totally committed to the one, not yet enamored of the other, but cognizant of both, Mozart's music gives unique expression to this spiritual crisis still unresolved today. Daemonically in Mozart the depths of cheerfulness and hopelessness interfuse as in redemptive suffering extremes of noncorrelation continue to reveal the glory of God. Throughout his life Luther felt tempted to confound the will of God with the voice of Satan. Listening to Mozart it is always hard to tell whether the heavens have opened up or the ground beneath our feet is about to cave in, or both. It is regrettable that Kierkegaard neglected to develop further his insight into the affinity of the aesthetic with the religious. If he had, he might have revised his estimate not only of Mozart's music but also of becoming a Christian. While Mozart takes irrepressible delight in illuminating the subtlest transitions of the inner life his music expresses beyond them our unstable lot on earth: at once ludicrous and pitiful, trying and uplifting, wretched and great. An age such as ours, reawakened to the bestial potentialities of civilized communities, may still find an element of regeneration in him who, two centuries after his death, confronts us, daemonically, with what we were at the outset and what we hope again to become at the end of time.

CHAPTER II

The Breakdown of Criticism:
Hume and Subjectivity

The Chevalier de Revel, envoy of Sardinia to the Hague, had [this] theory of the universe: "God died before finishing His work. His plans were magnificent and vast; His means were immense. The scaffolding, so to say, of His resources and appliances was in some measure complete when He perished. Everything which now exists was created for an end which no longer has existence. Ourselves, in particular, are aware of a destiny we cannot define. We are like watches without a dial, and the wheels wear themselves out with turning. They are endowed with intelligence, and, as they turn, incessantly repeat: 'I turn, I turn: therefore I serve some end.' I far prefer this folly to those of the Christians, Moslems, and philosophers of the first, sixth, and seventeenth centuries. . . . Good-bye, most dear and intelligent Wheel, who have the misfortune to be so superior to the clock you are part of, the clock that you derange."

Geoffrey Scott[1]

In his book on Hume[2] A. H. Basson argues that "the calm and resolved scepticism of the *Enquiry Concerning the Human Understanding*" rather than the knotted argumentation and progressively increasing stresses of the first Book of the *Treatise of Human Nature* represents the final position of the philosopher. To support this contention he quotes these celebrated passages. From the *Treatise:*

> Where am I, or what? From what causes do I derive my existence, and to what condition shall I return? Whose favour shall I court, and whose anger must I dread? What beings surround me? and on whom have

I any influence, or who have any influence on me? I am confounded with all these questions, and begin to fancy myself in the most deplorable condition imaginable, inviron'd with the deepest darkness, and utterly depriv'd of the use of every member and faculty.

But from the *Enquiry:*

If we take in our hand any volume; of divinity or school metaphysics, for instance; let us ask, Does it contain any abstract reasoning concerning quantity or number? No. Does it contain any experimental reasoning concerning matter of fact and existence? No. Commit it then to the flames; for it can contain nothing but sophistry and illusion.

This use of quotation seems both arbitrary and misleading. To begin with, Hume himself was never wholly satisfied with the notorious conclusion of the *Enquiry.* Had he been, it is hard to see why he would subsequently have written the *Dialogues Concerning Natural Religion.* The latter work abounds in statements that are far closer in spirit to the end of Book One of the *Treatise* than to the positivistic credo of the *Enquiry.* Like Kant, Hume could not bring himself to reject metaphysics as such. There are moments when he suggests such a repudiation, but they are not representative. In the *Dialogues* at any rate, Hume regards metaphysical questions in deadly earnest.

Even if Mr. Basson's reading of Hume were correct, it still would not follow that he had done justice to the direction of Hume's thought which, as is the case with all great thinkers, went beyond its immediate conclusions. In its influence on Kant and through him on Kierkegaard and the existentialists it opened up new approaches to old problems in addition to laying ghosts of man's speculative past. Hume's annihilation of deism did not in fact solely lead to atheism, but also posed such issues as the "truth of subjectivity" and the limitations of criticism as an end in itself. If his position in the *Dialogues* be closest to Philo's, then it attests to weaknesses as well as to the conventionally praised analytic powers of the skeptic. To be sure,

hen all has been said, Cleanthes has little to stand on,
emea is properly dispirited, and Philo—what does he
and *for*? Like Hume in one of his moods, he can amuse
imself and get "religion" out of his mind as a subject fit
ıly for the discharge of excess mental energy, but it is
ell-nigh inconceivable that Hume could long have re-
ained satisfied with such a solution. A conceptual frame-
ork that cannot accommodate some of man's most sig-
ficant experiences and aspirations leaves itself open to
ıe charge of triviality, and worse, of contempt. It would
ppear that Hume recognized this and wrote his *Dialogues*
ıt least of all to disclose the dangers of nihilism lurking
chind the ruins of dogmatism.

A participant's account of an event is invariably distinct
om a spectator's, much as the advice of a fellow sufferer
a concrete situation is apt to be more relevant than that
an outsider. One sphere where this difference emerges
ost sharply is in philosophies and histories of religion.
he so-called "objective" explorations reveal these features:
sinterestedness, universality of outlook, irony, playful-
ess, open-mindedness, and neutrality. Christianity, on
ch a view, would be regarded as another of the world's
ajor religions which has had a tremendous influence on
e development of civilization. What personal faith the
holar scrupulously examining the available evidence
olds himself becomes entirely tangential to his central
ncern—exact delineation. The appeal of the resulting
ork rests on its "dispassionate" elucidation of the issues.
ver against this approach must be placed the account
the "committed" writer. He too will utilize scholarly
pparatus, but there is no getting away from the fact that
: speaks a different language. By virtue of being a be-
ving Christian or believing enemy of Christianity he
ill not regard it as just another of the world's major
ligions. Not that he need become a proselytizer or dema-
gue, though his work will unavoidably disclose his stake
whatever is being discussed. Its most distinguishing
aracteristics are: authenticity, moral seriousness, par-
ularism, and stubbornness. No attempt is made to
parate the standpoint of the author from his material.

The reader is made to feel that he had to write about thi having received a kind of religious call to speak out.

Since the "committed" writer intimately knows his sul ject matter, having experienced it personally in son fashion, his books, inadequate as they may be in oth respects, will have a decided ring of forcefulness and i tensity. Paradoxical as the term may appear here, it precisely this kind of writing which possesses the greate "objectivity." For it is impossible to be objective abo something known only at a distance where the object description entails an experience inseparably linked to tl consciousness of the individual describing it. Take Hum treatment of religion—a seminal expression of Enlighte ment clarity and rigor. It is indeed tolerant, witty, ae thetically pleasant, and pervaded by Olympian calm All ecstasy and passion (though Hume knew better an said so) seem harnessed in the service of unbiased unde standing. The reader has a hard time deciding why Hun bothered to write about this particular subject. He skir the fringes, illuminates corners, cuts through superstru tures, but maintains the appearance of shrinking awa from the heart of his theme. In his treatment of miracl he remarks very truly: all eye-witness accounts must I mistrusted, especially where the phenomenon observed so extraordinary that it clashes with common sense. Hea ing the observation "there are blue swans in the pon one is justified in supposing that the observer's vision defective and his accustomed association of swans wi nonblueness confirmed. But in saying this, Hume miss the core of New Testament miracle situations where the witness had to express his faith in Christ before the could arise. Belief in a miracle in the context of the Go pels was never conceived as the culmination of an indu tive process, but as an ethical-religious commitment to a in a certain manner. Those who look on and in from tl outside will almost invariably show better judgment tha the participants, but at the price of authenticity.

Nevertheless, granting his Enlightenment terror of e thusiasm and his tendency to idolize reasonableness, in l *Dialogues Concerning Natural Religion* Hume transcen the issues that occasioned their composition. At first sight Cleanthes is defending "natural religion" from the "sifting, inquisitive disposition" of Philo to undermine all traditional values. Pious Demea, in this respect like Cleanthes, champions unsophisticated belief against free thought. Yet the disputes that arise between these two apologists for religious faith in opposition to skepticism are even more revealing than their agreement. What Hume presents us with is not the kind of simple discussion in which three individuals express diverse points of view and in which two are opposed to the third, but a genuinely dialectical situation where each perspective comes into separate collision with the others. Thus at the end of Part XI Cleanthes bitterly remarks that Philo has been calculating enough to be in league with Demea against him. Apart from the merits of this suspicion, the accumulating complexities of the argument (many of which escaped Cleanthes) no longer warrant the obvious dichotomy of belief and unbelief.

Hume's detachment from any concrete religious tradition while engendering the illusion that facts about God qualitatively equal other facts in history and nature, did not prevent him from coming to terms with the principal tensions in modern Christendom. Cleanthes is a man of little faith who claims to establish the Supreme Being by reversing the traditional formula *"credo ut intellegam"* and relying instead on the likeness of causes to their discernible effects: as if arguments, setting aside their coherence for the moment, could take the place of faith. Philo's celebrated rejoinder (causes and effects must resemble each other, nobody has ever experienced anything remotely comparable to the creation of the world, etc.), is juxtaposed with Cleanthes's persistent attempt to transform mysteries into problems. Ironically enough, it is his preposterous overestimate of the intellect in matters not wholly theoretical that has become distorted as the Humean heritage. Philo makes it quite plain to Cleanthes that whether the world be conceived as a machine or as an organism is from the religious point of view beside the point. In short, he destroys more than Cleanthes's arguments by attacking his attitude towards these arguments.

He ends up saying: Science and religion both have their respective autonomies, however much or little they overlap in particular instances.

Demea, on the other hand, is a typical fideist who, notwithstanding his lack of sophistication and dialectical skill, has a genuine feeling for the "evidence of things unseen." Modern men who have continued to believe, in part perhaps because their awareness of modernity did not cramp their way of living, share with Demea an over-simplified but sound conviction of what God means to them. In contrast there is Philo with his uncompromising separation of philosophical from Christian pursuits, his preference (to paraphrase James) for potential damnation over the threat of error, and his skepticism, which is to permeate virtually all religious philosophizing in the nineteenth and twentieth centuries. Philo's pessimism points ahead both to nihilism and the anguish of the existentialists. Thus Hume's three spokesmen are anything but stock rococo figures endowed at intervals by their creator with extraordinary powers of verbalization. Cleanthes's complacency suggests the eclipse of a live Christian culture; cynical Philo precariously traverses the never-never land of self-consuming criticism; and orthodox Demea is on the edge of entering a fundamentalist ivory tower. His self-righteousness coupled with Philo's irreverence and Cleanthes's temporizing pretty well define a world where nothing is sacred, enthusiasms come and go, and men take rain checks on their lives—in short, our world. In freely (perhaps unwittingly) acknowledging the short-comings of his antagonists, Hume in the *Dialogues* went far beyond the dispute over natural religion which was soon relieved, and exposed critical issues still alive today. Interpreters content to reiterate that Hume has never been answered in dealing the death blow to the varieties of rational theism miss another abiding aspect of his *Dialogues*, namely: the challenge to overcome the chasm between experience and knowledge with regard to truth so characteristic of post-Cartesian man.

In the present treatment of the *Dialogues* four aspects are particularly worth noting: first, Cleanthes's criticism of

Philo on the limits of skepticism; second, Cleanthes's and Demea's controversy over anthropomorphism in religion; third, Philo's and Demea's common ground of emotivism; and, finally, Philo's latent nihilism as at variance with the aspirations of Enlightenment naturalism. This focus on the dialectical interplay in the *Dialogues* is intended to correct the one-sided view of their place in the history of philosophy as an atheist manifesto. This interpretation follows a hint in Professor Basil Willey's latest volume of *Nineteenth Century Studies*[3] to the effect that "honest doubters" like Mark Rutherford (William Hale White) did far more for the survival of Christianity in modern England than many apologists. Quite possibly this further confirms the observation regarding the religious quality of Mozart's nonliturgical music: that some of the best Christian thinking since the seventeenth century has been done by "negative theologians" outside the Church. Hume might well have relished the role of God's advocate in rococo finery.

While Philo proves an indomitable detractor of natural religion and a clear-sighted critic of theological pretentiousness, the weakness of his position emerges when he is confronted by the religious consciousness in its more concrete manifestations. Cleanthes is quick to seize upon this weakness! "To erect religious faith on philosophical scepticism" may be an admirable occupation, particularly congenial to a placid temperament, but for the majority of mankind implicated in the precariousness of existence this is sheer talk:

> Though a man, in a flush of humour, after intense reflection on the many contradictions and imperfections of human reason, may entirely renounce all belief and opinion, it is impossible for him to persevere in this total scepticism or to make it appear in his conduct for a few hours. External objects press upon him; his philosophical melancholy dissipates; and even the utmost violence upon his temper will not be able, during any time, to preserve the poor appearance of scepticism.[4]

Whether or not philosophical skepticism dissipates depends on variables Cleanthes does not consider here, but surely he is correct in rejecting the skeptical mood as a sufficient condition for faith or even as a favorable antecedent. In the realm of religion no honest doubter appears to have found faith by doubt alone. The kind of life Kierkegaard led can only be accepted by the "exceptional individual" that he was, and even *he* sharply delineated the alternatives between mere "honesty" with its "sickness unto death" and "faith" with its "leap" into the arms of God. William James in expounding his "will to believe" [5] acknowledged that modern man would rather be damned and uncommitted to a false proposition than saved with the risk of being mistaken, at the same time insisting on this being an impossible state of affairs for most men to put up with indefinitely. The suspension of belief in crucial matters is untenable except for those prepared to drift. Philo's failure to realize anything like this rests on the typical Enlightenment bifurcation of passion and intellect. Such a divorce is precisely what a religious claim on an individual does not sanction. Where Cleanthes proves incompetent in defending a "reasonable" Christianity against the strictures of the very reason he deems thoroughly compatible with faith, his judgment of Philo's skepticism in the area of values is fundamentally sound. Either it becomes internally inconsistent by professing faith in spite of itself ("the sentiment of rationality") or, as Kierkegaard and Dostoevsky were to reveal later, it leads to nihilism.

Though the gulf between Philo and Cleanthes does in fact constitute the immediate occasion for the *Dialogues,* subsequent discussion is vitalized by the presence of Demea, who far from merely being an orthodox simpleton reiterating unanswerable pieties succeeds at times in making a better case than Cleanthes. Nor is his agreement with Philo on certain matters to be discounted as contrived for the sake of special pleading. It develops that the rift between the two believers can be of a deeper kind than that which separates the principal antagonists.

Hume here had a presentiment of the peculiar affinity existentialism and positivism came to have for each other:

It seems strange to me, said Cleanthes, that you, Demea, who are so sincere in the cause of religion, should still maintain the mysterious, incomprehensible nature of the Deity, and should insist so strenuously that he has no manner of likeness or resemblance to human creatures. The Deity, I can readily allow, possesses many powers and attributes of which we can have no comprehension; but, if our ideas, so far as they go be not just adequate and correspondent to his real nature, I know not what there is in this subject worth insisting on. Is the name, without any meaning, of such mighty importance? Or how do you mystics, who maintain the absolute incomprehensibility of the Deity, differ from sceptics or atheists, who assert that the first cause of all is unknown and unintelligible? Their temerity must be very great if, after rejecting the production by a mind—I mean a mind resembling the human (for I know no other)—they pretend to assign, with certainty, any other specific intelligible cause; and their conscience must be very scrupulous, indeed, if they refuse to call the universal unknown cause a God or Deity, and to bestow on him as many sublime eulogies and unmeaning epithets as you shall please to require of them.

Who could imagine, replied Demea, that Cleanthes, the calm philosophical Cleanthes, would attempt to refute his antagonists by affixing a nickname to them, and, like the common bigots and inquisitors of the age, have recourse to invective and declamation instead of reasoning? Or does he not perceive that these topics are easily retorted, and that *anthropomorphite* is an appellation as invidious, and implies as dangerous consequences, as the epithet of *mystic*, with which he has honoured us? In reality, Cleanthes, consider what it is you assert when you represent the Deity as similar to the human mind and understanding. . . .

Pray consider, said Philo, whom you are at present inveighing against [addressing Cleanthes]. You are honouring with the appellation of *atheist* all the sound, orthodox divines, almost, who have treated of this subject; and you will at last be, yourself, found, according to your reckoning, the only sound theist in the world. But if idolaters be atheists, as, I think, may justly be asserted, and Christian theologians the same, what becomes of the argument, so much celebrated, derived from the universal consent of mankind?[6]

This passage defines so well the dilemma that continues to perplex theist thinkers: if God is knowable, then he must be conceived in finite categories; if, on the other hand, God is hidden, then He transcends any intelligible formulation of His nature. Either God is knowable or He is hidden. Hence either He can be grasped by the reason or He remains an object of noncognitive faith. Many attempts, to be sure, have been made to take this dilemma by the horns or to escape through them, but they have all been unsuccessful for the simple reason that any solution presupposes a settlement of the very dispute around which the argument revolves. Thus the Incarnation is often adduced in support of the claim that through it immediacy and mystery become interfused, meaning (among other things) that God is at once revealed to and withdrawn from human apprehension. But this begs the question inasmuch as the Incarnation itself is a mystery, a paradox, as Kierkegaard put it, that constitutes an "offense" to the natural man.[7] The other way out is equally unsatisfactory. For if one maintains with Cleanthes "though it be allowed that the Deity possesses attributes of which we have no comprehension, yet we ought never to ascribe to him any attributes which are absolutely incompatible with that intelligent nature essential to him," [8] one sets oneself up as the authority that determines what God should be, a procedure contrary to the core of Biblical religion with its primary injunction that the Will of the Lord need not at all be commensurate with or open to approval by the will of His creatures.

In our own day, clearly, Cleanthes has lost ground to Demea. Largely owing to the genius of Kierkegaard in restating fundamental Biblical insights, and the tremendous influence of Karl Barth, current Protestant Christian thought virtually repudiates anthropomorphism. This by no means represents a solution of the dilemma, but rather affirms the legitimacy of paradox in a prophetic faith over against the claims of common sense. Whatever Christianity is *not,* it is unavoidably a mystery religion, and the mystery cannot be abolished without abolishing the religion. Anthropomorphic elements are either concessions to human inadequacy or an inherent part of the mystery itself. In any event, the complete humanization of theism as envisaged by Feuerbach is properly regarded as its annulment. The chasm between the human and divine which Cleanthes would not recognize becomes once again the backbone of Biblical faith. Meanwhile a prominent school of philosophy inspired by Hume has given unexpected support to this development in theology. "Whereof we cannot speak we must remain silent" can be interpreted as the philosophical justification of Demea's position. Since science cannot deal scientifically with values, it becomes legitimate to hold them on nonscientific grounds; in fact, this is the only way that we can hold them. What human beings generally regard as most meaningful is not transparent to verification procedures. But this need not be a calamity.[9] Wittgenstein and Barth have no quarrel on this point. Neither, thanks to Hume's perspicacity, did Philo and Demea. Agreement between skeptics and believers since the eighteenth century is essentially negative, rooted, as it were, in a common acceptance of the limitations of human reason to establish or invalidate faith.

Hume and Kierkegaard, great as are their differences in attitude and temperament, find themselves in ironic agreement on the inadequacy of reason and immediate experience to resolve religious problems. In his celebrated essay "On Miracles" Hume argues that the likelihood of their not having occurred is more convincing than the reliability of the witnesses on whose testimony they are believed. In *Training in Christianity* Kierkegaard maintains that to regard miracles as anything other than objects of faith twice removed from "immediacy" by the contradiction of

the God-man and "the possibility of offense" is blasphemy.
Hume also might have concurred with these propositions:

> For the proofs remain equivocal: they are the *pro et
> contra* of the reasoning intellect, and therefore can
> be used *contra et pro*. It is only by choice that the
> heart is revealed and surely it was for this cause
> Christ came into the world, that the thoughts of all
> hearts might be revealed, by the choice whether to
> believe or be offended.[10]

Unlike Kierkegaard, to be sure, Hume could not grasp the
"inside" of a Biblical miracle situation.

Hume, however, was keenly conscious of the varying
fortunes of skepticism in the history of Christianity:

> During ignorant ages [Philo remarks] such as those
> which followed the dissolution of the ancient schools,
> the priests perceived that atheism, deism, or heresy
> of any kind, could only proceed from the presumptu-
> ous questioning of received opinion, and from a be-
> lief that human reason was equal to everything. . . .
> But at present, when the influence of education is
> much diminished and men, from a more open com-
> merce of the world, have learned to compare the
> popular principles of different nations and ages, our
> sagacious divines have changed their whole system
> of philosophy and talk the language of Stoics, Pla-
> tonists, and Peripatetics, not that of Pyrrhonians and
> Academics. If we distrust human reason we now have
> no other principle to lead us into religion. Thus
> sceptics in one age, dogmatists in another. . . ."[11]

Note the irony of "sagacious divines," for Hume himself,
especially in the *Dialogues,* was aiding and abetting the
growing distrust of human reason which led to a new
understanding of skepticism within religion. This passage
in effect is a parody of Cleanthes's claim of contemporaneousness as if *he* knew what the score was to be. Philo and
Hume knew better.

This surprising note of unanimity between Philo and
Demea is struck again as they reflect together on the
misery and wickedness that pervade human experience.
To be sure, such a congenial theme has made bedfellows

of the greatest antagonists in the history of thought, yet it is apparent that their mutual sympathy on this score goes far beyond a conventional recital of complaints. Moreover, their adversary once again is Cleanthes, who characteristically tells them "if you can make out the present point, and prove mankind to be unhappy or corrupted, there is an end at once of all religion." [12] The Christendom against which Kierkegaard aimed his attack was of the same mind about this matter and so are most "adjusted" Protestants today. Hume was more realistic:

> It is my opinion, I own, replied Demea, that each man feels, in a manner, the truth of religion within his own breast, and, from a consciousness of his imbecility and misery rather than from any reasoning, is led to seek protection from that Being on whom he and all nature is dependent. So anxious or so tedious are even the best scenes of life that futurity is still the object of our hopes and fears. . . . I am indeed persuaded, said Philo, that the best and indeed the only method of bringing everyone to a due sense of religion is by just representations of the misery and wickedness of man. And for that purpose a talent of eloquence and strong imagery is more requisite than that of reasoning and argument. For is it necessary to prove what everyone feels within himself? It is only necessary to make us feel it, if possible, more intimately and sensibly. . . . Man, it is true, can by combination, surmount all his *real* enemies and become master of the whole animal creation; but does he not immediately raise up to himself imaginary enemies, the demons of his fancy, who haunt him with superstitious terrors and blast every enjoyment of life? [13]

Philosophical skepticism and Biblical religion find a common meeting ground in human feeling. Removed from the ordinary claims of verifiability, self-evident to all but the dehumanized, universally invoked and sung by the poets, it became throughout the nineteenth century the ideal authority for those who could not explain what they meant or had lost hope in saying anything meaningful about what agitated them the most. Contrary to the optimistic rationalism of Cleanthes, the preservation and efficacy of religion in the lives of individuals (as well as in cultures) can largely be accounted for by its satisfaction of the perennial human need for reassurance, purification, and hope amidst the dread and perplexities of Being. Were mankind innocent and happy it would have nothing to crave for, no ideal to set off from the way things are, and religion would disappear. It is precisely the contingencies of life which make men question their own self-sufficiency and turn to God.[14]

But feeling by itself (like skepticism) is no dependable guide to religious truth. This was one of the painful discoveries made by the Romantics. The intuitive apprehension of wickedness and misery is as compatible with nihilism as with the acceptance of any body of revealed truth. Schopenhauer's will not to will follows as naturally from an acute sensitivity to the dynamics of will as does Nietzsche's "will to power." Philo and Demea do well to stress the emotive character and roots of religious faith over against the prevailing intellectualism embodied in Cleanthes and not uncongenial to Hume himself, but they tend to overlook the importance of decision, which cannot be reduced to either feeling or intellect. As James was to emphasize, a man's religious faith bears witness primarily to how he lives and acts, rather than to what he thinks or feels. The great problem for modern philosophy has been to square a purely quantitative account of reality, devoid of any intrinsic significance for human hopes and fears, with the Occidental passion for meaningfulness in historical events. "Feeling," "dialectical necessity," "progress," "evolution"—all these were used as categories to bridge the gap between fact and value, but to no avail. Only the fanatics (the Marxists, for instance) solved the problem by making it appear nonexistent. The mystics continued to wonder whether they were in touch with something not merely symbolically real, hence in all likelihood a private or public illusion, and the skeptics continued their quest for principles of choice and action that if found would prove themselves metaskeptical. Risk as a regulative concept for existential choice is (for all practical purposes) a twentieth-century notion.

Philo's radical skepticism linked to "subjectivism" in matters of value foreshadows, particularly in one respect, the varieties of nihilism that began to appear early in the nineteenth century. He is not yet the militant type of nihilist who openly declares that God is dead or that without him everything becomes permissible, nor does he inveigh against every type of order for being "artificial" or (which is far from unrelated) condone every type of order as circumstantially justified. The spiritual crisis of Western man had on the whole not penetrated quite so deeply, though Hume must have sensed its coming. Strictly speaking, the *Dialogues* never question the existence of the Deity, but repudiate the possibility of establishing His nature. Yet when Philo comes to speak of evil in the world he reveals himself typically existential in that inequities strike him far more forcefully than the rational aspects in reality. St. Augustine's confidence in the ultimate harmony of all things under God as well as Leibniz's grandiose attempt to reconcile necessity with desirability have vanished.

Here is Philo describing the state of the world:

The world, for aught he [anyone] knows, is very faulty and imperfect, compared to a superior standing, and was only the first rude essay of some infant deity who afterwards abandoned it, ashamed of his lame performance; it is the work only of some dependent, inferior deity, and is the object of derision to his superiors; it is the production of old age and dotage in some superannuated deity, and ever since his death has run on at adventures, from the first impulse and active force which it received from him. Look around the universe. What an immense profusion of beings, animated and organized, sensible and active! You admire this prodigious variety and fecundity. But inspect a little more narrowly these living existences, the only beings worth regarding. How hostile and destructive to each other! How insufficient all of them for their own happiness! How contemptible or odious to the spectator! *The whole presents nothing but the idea of blind nature, impregnated by a great vivifying principle, and pouring forth from her lap, without discernment or parental care, her maimed and abortive children!* [15]

No atheist existentialist has given a more negative estimate of man's condition than that. Both man and the external world are regarded as abandoned, sacrificed, so to speak, to the capriciousness of indifferent forces. Not only is there no enduring preponderance of good over evil (as in Augustine), but even the Manichaean hypothesis of a perennial conflict between the two up to a Last Judgment in favor of the former is repudiated for a hypothesis that conceives the first cause of the universe to "have neither goodness nor malice."

Just as a child would on occasion prefer punishment to being ignored, so the acceptance of total nonpurposiveness as "by far the most probable hypothesis" is on the part of Western man tantamount to spiritual suicide. Such a position is contrary to every authentic form of Judaism and Christianity as well as being in conflict with the belief in history as a meaningful pattern of events leading to a specific consummation, a belief as necessary for the "scientific" specialist as for religious orthodoxy, not to mention the vast majority in the West today who profess a vague but often impassioned hope in the progress of their country, civilization, or way of living.[16] Its fundamental contradiction to the over-all Western tradition does not of course invalidate Philo's stand. Rather it shows that the tradition was already dying in the keenest mind of the eighteenth century. Philo's point of view here anticipates the existential experience of "downward transcendence" as exemplified in Kafka's "Penal Colony."

The contrast between Job, who continued to argue with God in spite of every discouragement visited upon him, and Philo, who schizophrenically acquiesces in a meaningless world that his feelings cannot bear, defines the predicament of Enlightenment sensibility. Fairly tranquil conditions (at least for the minority to which Hume belonged) still allowed him to rely on periodic distraction at the billiard table where, as he informs us in the *Treatise,* the philosopher gives himself up to less gloomy reflections than those that preoccupy him in his study. Unfortunately, perhaps, the permanent possibilty of such diversion has since been shattered, especially for the thinking man. In reflection, at any rate, Hume could hardly avoid touching the abyss that his successors either wallowed in, struggled to conquer or dishonestly evaded. *The Dialogues Concerning Natural Religion* are free from the scars of direct identification with the human predicament which, characterize the works of John Wesley and Dr. Johnson, and, a little later, of Kierkegaard, but indeed they testify to Hume's genius in discerning the signs of his times.[17]

CHAPTER III

The Breakdown of Empirical Certainty: William James and the Leap

If I say that we are compelled to consider the world *as if* it were the work of a Supreme Understanding and Will, I really say nothing more than that a watch, a ship, a regiment, bears the same relation to the watchmaker, the shipbuilder, the commanding officer as the world of sense (or whatever constitutes the substratum of this complex of appearances) does to the unknown, which I do not hereby know as it is in itself but as it is for me, that is, in relation to the world of which I am a part.

Immanuel Kant[1]

There is a curious parallel in the history of thought between the complete identification of Hume's influence with positivism and twentieth-century analytic philosophy, and the simple juxtaposition of William James with pragmatism. The appeal of half-truths being so much greater than that of lies, it is not surprising that these one-sided interpretations have survived down to the present day. Hume the destroyer of philosophical nonsense and James the spiritual fountainhead of American "do it yourself" present Anglo-American philosophers with a respectable image of themselves laboring in a great tradition. And of course it is perfectly legitimate to regard Hume and James as empiricists fighting the obscurantism of their respective generations, provided that this view is not presented as exhaustive. For as Hume led to Kant as well as to A. J. Ayer, James said many things unheeded by John Dewey. What links Hume to James is not merely a common aversion to useless speculation, but the Kantian quest for the possibility of meaningful answers to ultimate questions. Hume leaves Philo unreconciled both to atheism and dogmatic rational theology; Kant provides him with regulative ideas of the practical reason; Kierkegaard invites him to take the Christian Leap; and William James, availing himself of the tools of phenomenological analysis, argues for the legitimacy, apart from a prior religious commitment, of the Leap.

James the laboratory psychologist and radical empiricist lives on in the idolatry of science still permeating the American scene, but James the critic of this idolatry, the early champion of Freud, the founder of an existentialist-phenomenological method in value philosophy has been woefully neglected, save in such odd places as Husserl's *Ideenlehre*.[2] Moreover, James the lover of adventure and rugged individualism was appropriated by "popular sooth-sayers" and "religious utilitarians," but James the critic of industrial civilization, the enemy of materialism who sounded many a Melvillean note to his contemporaries, virtually died with them. His death coincided with the last era of untroubled hopefulness, before the years when the First World War, the Roaring Twenties, the Depression, the Second World War, and the Cold War transformed the image of the American dream into a potential nightmare.

Where Dewey appears to have regarded the myth of the open road as a permanent possibility if not an ideal model for all mankind, James early realized the inadequacy of enlightened liberalism for the impending mass age. The emphasis in his philosophy as in the unusual family group in which he grew up is on the individual—the eccentric minority. However, the contribution of the tenets of pragmatism to American education may one day be evaluated, it is certain that James himself would have been horrified by the cult of mediocrity and materialism drawing support from his reputation. Finally, *The Varieties of Religious Experience*, which became a classic text in comparative religion, is something besides an apology for cranks: it is a far-searching study of the relationship between the prosaic and the daemonic in the realm of

Erlebnis, with the Dostoevskian-Freudian thesis that the two are implicated in each other, however antithetical as abstractions. Together with psychoanalysis and Dostoevsky's psychological realism James's *Varieties* represents a milestone in the conquest of Cartesian dualism.

Thoroughly grounded in his family tradition of dinnertable dialectics, James throughout his life remained a wanderer both in the physical and intellectual sense of the term. On the one hand, there were his frequent trips to Europe with exposure to currents of thought virtually unknown in the United States at that time; on the other, his irreconcilable attraction to and repulsion from the laboratory. Much can be made of the Swedenborgian influence his father exercised on him (though he never admitted fully understanding him) or of the strained affection he felt for his brother with its undertones of American-European rivalry. There is also James's indebtedness to Pascal and (vicariously, at any rate) to St. Augustine, thinkers, incidentally, who were not exactly *en vogue* at late nineteenth-century Harvard. But possibly of greater import for his over-all philosophical development than any purely intellectual influences was his own temperament. As the author of "The Sentiment of Rationality" would have been the first to admit, no factor plays a more prominent role in determining the character of philosophical thinking than the philosopher's character. And James, in spite of a Theodore Roosevelt streak of militant strenuousness in his make-up, was a manic depressive subject to all the disintegrating and elevating effects of that condition. Again and again he enthusiastically espouses such values as courage, risk-taking, and enterprise with an almost fanatical insistence on not giving up the fight, however ominous the odds. In his diary Gorky refers to some very negative opinions James expressed about Russia in 1905.[3] Among other things, the author of the *Varieties* was puzzled and somewhat irritated by the abnormal souls of Dostovesky, so different from what "we" are used to in the West. When talking to teachers and students James had little patience with those who hesitated in responding to great challenges. Unlike his brother Henry, William would not withdraw into a precious environment nor was he insufficiently endowed with the American pioneer spirit to relapse into gloom. But the affirmative note that he struck for his readers and listeners did not come easily to him. It grew out of great personal pain, the struggling response of a "twice-born" personality to the horrors of being:

> Now, my dear little girl [writing to his daughter many years after his great spiritual crisis in Berlin], you have come to an age when the inward life develops and when some people (and on the whole those who have most of a destiny) find that all is not a bed of roses. Among other things there will be waves of terrible sadness, which last sometimes for days; and dissatisfaction with one's self, and irritation at others, and anger at circumstances and stony insensibilities, etc. etc., which taken together form a melancholy. Now, painful as it is, this is sent to us for an enlightenment. It always passes off, and we learn about life from it, and we ought to learn a great many good things if we react on it rightly. . . . Many persons take a kind of sickly delight in hugging it; and some sentimental ones may even be proud of it, as showing a fine sorrowful kind of sensibility. Such persons make a regular habit of the luxury of woe. That is the worst possible reaction on it. . . . The worst of it often is that, while we are in it, we don't *want* to get out of it. We hate it, and yet we prefer staying in it— that is a part of the disease. If we find ourselves like that, we must make ourselves do something different, go with people, speak cheerfully, set ourselves to some hard work, make ourselves sweat, etc.; and that is the good way of reacting that makes of us a valuable character. The disease makes you think of *yourself* all the time; and the way out of it is to keep as busy as we can thinking of *things* and of other people—no matter what's the matter with our self. . . . [4]

And also, this letter to his dying sister, unique for its unmitigated frankness and high degree of self-revelation:

Dearest Alice. . . . Of course [this medical verdict of your case may mean] as all men know, a finite length of days; and then, good-bye to neurasthenia and neuralgia and headache, and weariness and palpitation and disgust all at one stroke—I should think you would be reconciled to the prospect with all its pluses and minuses! I know you've never cared for life, and to me, now at the age of nearly fifty, life and death seem singularly close together in all of us—and life a mere farce of frustration in all, so far as the realization of the innermost goal to which we are made respectively capable of feeling an affinity and responding. Your frustrations are only rather more flagrant than the rule; and you've been saved many forms of self-dissatisfaction and misery which appertain to such a multiplication of responsible relations to different people as I, for instance, have got into. . . . It may seem odd for me to talk to you in this cool way about your end, but, my dear little sister, if one has things present to one's mind, and I know they are present enough to your mind, why not speak them out? I am sure you appreciate that best. How many times I have thought, in the past year, when my days were so full of strong and varied impressions and activities, of the long unchanging hours in bed which those days stood for with you, and wondered how you bore the slow-paced monotony at all, as you did! You can't tell how I've pitied you. But you *shall* come to your rights ere long. Meanwhile take things gently. . . .[5]

Throughout his writings, notwithstanding their apparent vigor and good spirits, James shows a remarkable affinity for the darker aspects of existence. This affinity is so striking precisely because of its antithetical character to the normal *joie de vivre* of the New World. Not for him the implicit antinomianism in "neo-orthodoxy" with its ironies of human history as implicated in the works of the devil. Nineteenth-century thinkers like Heine, Kierkegaard, Burckhardt, Flaubert, and Nietzsche had expressed revulsion and disgust for a civilization they sensed to be dying. Their reflections anticipated a religious vacuum crying out for a "new being." This is not quite yet the case with James. Contrary to his brother, he was endowed with a sparkling facility for coming to terms with unconventional situations and with a great capacity for relish and exuberance. Not unaffected by the religious crisis in Christendom, he continues to identify himself for the most part with Thoreauian individualism and the moral earnestness of a Channing, a practical philosophy (whatever its theoretical limitations) justly noted for its spirit of adventure, open-mindedness, and disregard of accepted precedents. And yet, the same William James who infused his writings with a kind of Whitmanesque love of life discloses himself, and not only in *The Varieties of Religious Experience,* as an authentic commentator on the unstable, intransigent, and double-edged facets of experience.

Whilst in this state of philosophic pessimism and general depression of spirits about my prospects, I went one evening into a dressing-room in the twilight, to procure some article that was there; when suddenly there fell upon me without any warning, just as if it came out of the darkness, a horrible fear of my own existence. Simultaneously there arose in my mind the image of an epileptic patient whom I had seen in the asylum, a black-haired youth with greenish skin, entirely idiotic, who used to sit all day on one of the benches, or rather shelves, against the wall, with his knees drawn up against his chin, and the coarse gray undershirt, which was his only garment, drawn over them, inclosing his entire figure. He sat there like a sort of sculptured Egyptian cat or Peruvian mummy, moving nothing but his black eyes and looking absolutely non-human. This image and my fear entered into a species of combination with each other. *That shape am I,* I felt, potentially. Nothing that I possess can defend me against that fate, if the hour for it should strike for me as it struck for him. There was such a horror of him, and such a perception of my own merely momentary discrepancy from him, that it was as if something hitherto solid within my breast gave way entirely, and I became a mass of quivering fear. After this the universe was changed for me altogether. I woke morning after morning with a horrible dread at the pit of my stomach, and with a sense of the insecurity of life that I never knew before, and that I have never felt since. It was like a revelation; and although the immediate feelings passed away, the experience has made me sympathetic with the morbid feelings of others ever since. It gradually faded, but for months I was unable to go out in the dark alone.

In general I dreaded to be left alone. I remember wondering how other people could live, how I myself had ever lived, so unconscious of that pit of insecurity beneath the surface of life. My mother in particular, a very cheerful person, seemed to me a perfect paradox in her unconsciousness of danger, which you may well believe I was very careful not to disturb by revelations of my own state of mind. I have always thought that this experience of melancholia of mine had a religious bearing. . . . I mean that the fear was so invasive and powerful that, if I had not clung to scripture texts like *The eternal God is my refuge,* etc., *Come unto me all ye that labor and are heavy-laden,* etc., *I am the Resurrection and the Life,* etc., I think I should have grown really insane.[6]

The very terminology he uses strikingly resembles the "existential" vocabulary of Kierkegaard and his twentieth-century disciples. Thus he speaks of *fringe of consciousness, scientism, concrete thinker, gossip of the universe, interested spectator, one-sided champion of special ideals, unique situation, existential facts, existential study, the entire man, the ontological wonder-sickness, peace of rationality, ontological emotion, speculative melancholy, haunting sense of futurity, eternal void, fundamental ground for seriousness, risk . . . beyond the literal evidence, launching oneself in a moment of despair, the use of the subjective method, the lonely emergencies of life, purely inward forces, a nameless* Unheimlichkeit, *a stake in the unknown, gleams of the awful and the infinite, unconquerable subjectivity,* and *human nature in extremis.* Moreover, the titles of such philosophical essays as "On a Certain Blindness in Human Beings," "Is Life Worth

Living," "What Makes a Life Significant," "The Importance of Individuals," "On Some Hegelisms," "The Sentiment of Rationality," and "The Will to Believe" are consonant with the Kierkegaardian *Stages on Life's Way, The Concept of Dread,* and *Concluding Unscientific Postscript.*

Also relevant in this connection is James's pointed dislike of academicians and their gatherings. Like Kierkegaard, Schopenhauer, and Nietzsche he felt strongly that philosophers do their best thinking in solitude. This attitude was coupled with an over-all distrust of the theoretical divorced from the practical. His partiality to homespun and colloquial expressions, his preference for one-hour talks to students which he hesitated to commit to paper (reminiscent of Kierkegaard's *Edifying Discourses* delivered informally of a Sunday afternoon—after church was over), his fondness for choosing instances of familiar experience (*Does the man go round the squirrel or not?*) to illustrate metaphysical problems, his disarming candor—all these are features often associated with existentialist deliberation. James carried his learning lightly. Perhaps this questioning of intellectuality is one of the necessary conditions for a new philosophy:

> But surely you must admit that since there must be professors in the world, Wundt is the most praiseworthy and never-too-much-to-be-respected type of the species. He isn't a genius, he is a *professor*—a being whose duty is to know everything, and have his own opinion about everything, connected with his *Fach.* Wundt has the most prodigious faculty for appropriating and preserving knowledge, and as for opinions, he takes *au grand serieux* his duties there. He says of each possible subject, "Here I must have an opinion. Let's see! What shall it be? How many possible opinions are there? three? four? Yes! just four! Shall I take one of these? It will seem more original to take a higher position, a sort of *Vermittelungsansicht* between them all. That I will do, etc., etc." So he acquires a complete assortment of opinions of his own; and, as his memory is so good, he seldom forgets which they are! But this is not

reprehensible; it is admirable—from the professorial point of view. To be sure, one gets tired of that point of view after awhile. But was there ever, since Christian Wolff's time, such a model of the German Professor? He has utilized to the utmost fibre every gift that Heaven endowed him with at his birth, and made of it all that mortal pertinacity could make. . . .[7]

In speaking of the function of philosophy James stresses its affinity with poetry and its chief relevance to the inner life. Although exercising a lifelong interest in experimental medicine and psychology, unlike so many philosophers in the Anglo-Saxon tradition he never acknowledged science as the paradigm of all rational activity. On the one hand, he protests against the excessive claims of metaphysics, suggesting that to look at things under the aspect of eternity is beyond the power of any man. It follows that there are certain incongruities and antinomies in our experience to which even thought must bow. The philosopher, far from being a manifestation of Hegelian World Spirit who with Olympian calm looks down upon his erring fellow creatures and sets them right, stands just as they do, involved in the tempestuous course of events. Only finite perspectives are accessible to contingent beings. If the philosopher is not free from the perils of precarious existence that are the historical lot of the human race, his role becomes the more modest one of illuminating perplexities, pointing the way, and deepening our view of things by showing us how differently they look when seen in different lights. On the other hand, James's ontological humility and devotion to the humanly discernible must be sharply distinguished from the positivistic canons of simplicity and transparency. While he repudiated the apodictic assertions of pre- and post-Kantian metaphysics, he rejected neither the possibility nor the necessity of dealing with these selfsame issues in another way. Why should philosophic propositions express scientific truth if they are intended to convey meanings that have little to do with science? Since the subject matter of poets and philosophers has more in common than the subject matter of philosophers and scientists, it would seem only proper that the work of a philosopher should, in part at any rate, be recognized as a poetic achievement with all its inherent deficiencies and virtues. It is tempting to suppose that James's preoccupation with philosophy as *Geisteswissenschaft* rather than *Naturwissenschaft* was influenced by his youthful encounter with Dilthey in Berlin. In any event, he refused to take the position that philosophical understanding because it cannot attain the precision of scientific theory must therefore be consigned to something at best dispensable in a pinch. What he did essentially was to substitute tentativeness for certainty, concrete universality for a priori abstractness, intersubjectivity for impersonal oneness, and immediate concern for disinterested detachment.[8]

So far as his "subjectivism" is concerned, it is first of all (as in Kierkegaard and Nietzsche) an attack on intellectual pretentiousness. What James could not abide was scientism—an uncritical devotion to "scientific objectivity" in *all* matters, under the pretext of personal disinterestedness. "The Sentiment of Rationality" (as well as "The Will to Believe") explodes the notion that what goes under the name of scientific or rational approach to the fundamental issues of human existence is *ipso facto* any more authentic or encompassing than rival points of view. In fact, James (here again like Kierkegaard) proceeds to suggest that being scientific in the sense of basing one's outlook (*Weltanschauung*) on the hypotheses of science is one among many sentiments operative in human nature, and so far as certain questions are concerned a most inadequate sentiment indeed. Where an impersonal view is called for, where we are not required to take a stand, where in effect we are prepared to define objectivity as the minimum participation of the individual in the results of his deliberations—in counting chickens, getting a fair sample of public opinion, or working out theoretical problems in mathematics, there science rules supreme. Of course, as James makes very clear in "The Will to Believe," there have arisen great tensions between the claims of empirical evidence and other claims devolving upon us which this evidence by itself is unable to corroborate or refute. But life is full of tensions in any event, and it is arbitrary to assume that in the name of science they will all be relieved. The questions that the extreme analysts regard as meaningless because they cannot answer them within their particular framework continue to be the questions that bother humanity (including the analysts), and only the most perverse reasoning would lead to the conclusion that for the sake of the tyranny of science they be dropped from human discourse.

Subjectivity in James therefore is not, as commonly supposed, a mere indulgence in personal nostalgia or contrariety to technical philosophy under the guise of maintaining an elevated tone, but the acknowledgment of a tremendous chasm separating problems of comparatively little import to the inner man from those that do not permit the inquirer to "forget" himself in his inquiries. And it is a profound insight of James that certain answers we seek are never ready-given through calculation but only disclose themselves gradually in the wake of personal choice. That each man's philosophy is unavoidably determined by the kind of man he is, even where the correspondence appears paradoxical, is no longer a novel notion, yet it should be remembered that James saw and developed some of its multifarious implications considerably before phenomenology, psychoanalysis, and *Daseinsanalyse* made their impact.[9]

James recognizes an irreducible tension between the speculative incentive for monistic simplicity and the willingness to know things as they are for us who must come to terms with them; he himself indicates a decided preference for the Job-like existentialist approach to basic philosophical problems without losing sight of its limitations and its due supplementation by the other. To want to see the world as a cosmos is intrinsically as valid a sentiment as beholding it as a conglomeration of discontinuous facts, so long as the intelligibility imputed to these facts is not absolutized. Do not, in fact, these two veins running concurrently through Augustine's thought account for its perennial vitality and depth? When, however, as happened with modern classical philosophy, the spectator simply eclipses the participant in reflection, with *Erlebnis* disappearing in *Verstand,* philosophy is out of joint. And there is no reason, really, why the participant cannot argue the concrete as rationally as the spectator can contemplate the distant with awareness of his ties to contingency.[10]

While James's insistence on intersubjectivity and concreteness is pervasive,[11] nowhere else in his writings does it attain the intensity and depth of "The Will to Believe." No problem has received more attention in recent value philosophy than the dynamics of decision. Whether it be the religious existentialists "deciding" for God or the nonreligious existentialists "deciding" for humanity or the void, the precarious line separating doubt and commitment, freedom and responsibility, and aloofness and interest has become the Rubicon of our age. Not only the origin and goal of decision, but the strategy and tactics by which it is arrived at, postponed, avoided, reversed (where possible), and forfeited are now objects of diverse types of inquiry. In addition to a general revival of fideism in Protestant theology and the peculiar ideological strains and stresses of the twentieth century, an intrinsic reason for this development is the convergence of objectivity and subjectivity around the phenomenon of choice. The problem of decision at once throws into sharp relief objectively discernible evidence (the situation in which the agent finds himself) as well as individual response to this situation. Thus Kierkegaard demonstrated with impressive clarity how and why certain modes of existence become inauthentic for certain individuals in certain circumstances, but he could not show why a "leap" into the arms of the Christian God is universally more compelling than irreligious pessimism. Beyond his insistence on an inescapable Either/Or for one who is trying to become a Christian he could not go. Similarly, James's argument in "The Will to Believe" is above all a description of a state of mind which cannot be relieved of its insecurity by the act of suspended judgment. Objectively, James spells out the conditions under which intellectual or spiritual neutrality becomes literally impossible. Subjectively, he would rather take his chances by hoping for a better world than this, but whether or not such a world exists is in effect tangential to his central point: *man on very special occasions must choose irrevocably!*

Like so many classical expressions of anti-Cartesian thought, James's "Will to Believe" is essentially a protest, in this instance against a misuse of scientific method in a crucial chapter of William Clifford's *Lectures and Essays* entitled "The Ethics of Belief." According to Clifford, discernible evidence is the highest tribunal of modern (enlightened man) in the light of which he should make all his decisions. If the evidence affecting a particular question such as religion is inadequate either pro or con, then he must suspend judgment, just as a scientist will not publish the results of an experiment unless he is sure of sufficient substantiating data. James's refutation of Clifford has a significance far deeper than most commentators suspect. For it is not merely the latter's view of science and its scope of relevance that he calls into question, but a seminal religious position of the modern intellectual which was not alien to James himself. This position is conventionally known as agnosticism.[12]

Agnosticism is a state of mind in which you do not take sides on an issue because you are not inwardly compelled to do so. Your explanation of this attitude may be "lack of evidence," but why make so much fuss about evidence unless you believe in it religiously? The certainty with which "agnostics" have taken stands on the most complex political and social issues belies such a faith. Their suspension of judgment on matters of traditional religion was not solely, as is commonly supposed, a natural consequence of supreme allegiance to empirical fact, but a decision—with its historical roots in the gradual secularization of life since the Renaissance—to leave supernaturalism to those who needed it for want of sufficient clear-sightedness. For agnostics in the nineteenth century it was no longer as easy to relegate religion to "morality tinged with emotion"—a convenient buttress for public-spiritedness and virtue or a haven for the ignorant. Professor Willey's "honest doubters" (who are actually close to James) had once again become far too bothered by the "establishment" to tolerate it with that mixture of disdain and wit so admirably maintained by Voltaire. At the same time, tormented and aroused as they were, their torment was still not intense enough for them to reject Christianity like Nietzsche or to espouse it paradoxically like Kierkegaard. William James himself, while temperamentally predisposed to be among the "saving remnant," was never provoked to follow the extremes of the greatest thinkers of the age. But he remained that rare phenomenon among modern skeptics: a pluralist who was able to put his finger on the basic weakness of unrequited openmindedness, however satisfying it might temporarily appear to the intellectual torn between his allegiance to empirical evidence and his nostalgia for the word of God.

James's "Will to Believe" was meant to deal the death blow to dishonest doubt—the kind of doubt that becomes internally inconsistent in relation to its object, like devising a test for trustworthiness. The individual who sets out to confirm the worthiness of his trust of another, by virtue of this very design has already broken it. Analogously, James is saying, the skeptic who asks for proof of religious faith thereby indicates a lack of faith. This is particularly true of the idolater of science, whose devotion to calculation and facts in the realm of personal experience betrays an ill-concealed fear of freedom. "The Will to Believe" is the outstanding American contribution to the growing literature on the dreadfulness of freedom. Criticism of this essay, with Kierkegaardian irony, invariably misses the point. The frightening subjectivity to which James presumably gives license is really much less frightening in the twentieth century than the distorted image of the statistical man which is subjected to such brilliant examination. For the enemy of the "will to believe" was never the dedicated scientist, but the man (so familiar in our midst) who submits his destiny to the expert planning of guidance counselors. When man wants to live a predictable life he ceases to be human. This is James's timely theme in "The Will to Believe." [13]

St. Augustine in his *Confessions* already came close to the heart of James's argument:

> I found nothing in [St. Ambrose's] teachings that offended me, though I could not yet know for certain whether what he taught was true. For all this time I restrained my heart from assenting to anything, fearing to fall headlong into error. Instead, *by this hanging in suspense, I was being strangled.* For my desire was to be as certain of invisible things as I was that seven and three are ten. I was not so deranged as to believe that this could not be comprehended, but my desire was to have other things as clear as this, whether they were physical objects which were not present to my senses, or spiritual objects, which I did not know how to conceive of except in physical terms. . . . *If I could have believed, I might have been cured,* and with the sight of my soul cleared up, it might in some way have been directed toward thy truth, which always abideth and fails in nothing. But, just as it happens that a man who has tried a bad physician fears to trust himself with a good one, so it was with the health of my soul, which could not be healed except by believing. *But lest it should believe falsehoods, it refused to be cured,* resisting thy hand, who has prepared for us the medicines of faith and applied them to the maladies of the whole world, and endowed them with such great efficacy. . . . O Lord, little by little, with a gentle and most merciful hand, drawing and calming my heart, thou didst persuade me that, if I took into account the multitude of things I had never seen, nor been present when they were enacted—such as many of the events of secular history; and the numerous reports of places and cities which I had not seen; or such as my relations with many friends, or physicians, or with these men and those—*that unless we should believe, we should do nothing at all in this life.* Finally, I was impressed with what an unalterable assurance I believe which two people were my parents, though this was impossible for me to know otherwise than by hearsay. . . .[14]

With regard to situations where human beings find it impossible to remain neutral and where the available evidence on which to make a decision is not clear-cut, it is justifiable to choose that alternative promising the greatest degree of happiness or the greatest mitigation of unhappiness. For any other course of action under such circumstances would be no more solidly grounded in "objectivity." James assumes here (undoubtedly with undue neglect of the "death instinct" and Zen) that individuals prefer potential happiness to misery. But to attribute to him the view that people are warranted in believing anything they please is utter nonsense: the "will to believe" situation only covers a very small range of choices human beings are called upon to make. If and only if the option be forced is (so far as the religious question is concerned) a decision for belief over unbelief justified. The notion of "forced option" by itself is revealing. According to James's terminology, options may and usually do consist of hypotheses that are dead, trivial, or unforced—meaning that they do not confront the individual with live alternatives to choose from, that he can take a disinterested stand outside these alternatives, and that if he makes up his mind he may change it, undo what he did, and start contemplating the original possibilities afresh as if meanwhile nothing had transpired.

For a true understanding of James's argument it should be emphasized that unless the alternatives are experienced by the individual as making an inescapable claim upon him, irrespective of their "objective" merits they will not qualify existentially. The fact that believing Christians are not apt to be torn between Buddhism and Mohammedanism, for example, does not affect the truth value of these religious traditions, but sets them off for *Christians* as abstract modes of thought rather than concrete possibilities. What does not concern me personally may be (historically speaking) far more important than what does, but then what does not concern me personally does not really matter for me and hence requires no personal decision. Like Kierkegaard and in opposition to sociological determinism, James felt that some answers can only be authentic for the individual who accepts them as true *for him*. This is not intended to obscure the many other types of choice we humans must make. James did not intend us to consult "The Will to Believe" in picking a refrigerator brand.

While most options are not genuine in the sense of being forced, momentous, and live, the majority remain unique opportunities. No "moment" returns exactly as it was. Nevertheless, it is obvious that much of the time we can resolve dilemmas of choice without having or needing to have recourse to the radical stratagems of "The Will to Believe." In his essay James specifically addresses himself to the religious crisis of his, and for that matter, still of our day. His argument rests on the deliberately articulated premise that the choice between Christianity and free thought continues to be a genuine option for Western man which, as it were, engages him completely, demands a decisive answer, and will never come again in the same form. Interestingly enough, James himself never questioned the truth of this assumption, though in the light of his contemporary situation it was no longer self-evident. Kierkegaard, Marx, Nietzsche, and Dostoevsky had already taken the "death of God" seriously either as a possibility to be dreaded for the inner life or as a desideratum of a "new order." But it is one thing to re-mark in criticism of "The Will to Believe" that James underestimated the post-Christian character of his times; another, to demonstrate that this poor historical judgment undermines his central position regarding forced options. James no doubt took too much for granted in viewing Christianity as *the* live religious hypothesis for his con-temporaries.[15] Their alienation from what theists tra-ditionally believed had progressed to a point where it might have been more apt to use Schopenhauer's "nirvana" or Adler's "ethical culture." Yet it is hard to see how this false estimate could affect the validity of James's central thesis that empirical certainty is an absurd criterion for religious faith, not only because such certainty eludes our grasp but also because of the nature of human freedom with its correlative precariousness of all deeper commit-ment.

More clearly than any evolutionist or transcendentalist

of his day he understood the inescapability of risk in human affairs:

> *Better risk loss of truth than chance of error*—that is your faith-vetoer's exact position. He is actively playing his stake as much as the believer; he is backing the field against the religious hypothesis, just as the believer is backing the religious hypothesis against the field. To preach scepticism to us as a duty until "sufficient evidence" for religion be found, is tantamount therefore to telling us, when in the presence of the religious hypothesis, that to yield to our fear of its being error is wider and better than to yield to our hope that it may be true. *It is not intellect against all passions then; it is only intellect with one passion laying down its law.* And by what, forsooth, is the supreme wisdom of this passion warranted? Dupery for dupery, what proof is there that dupery through hope is so much worse than dupery through fear? [16]

Cartesian man would rather be damned than fall into error. Why is it, James asks himself, that the fear of hell has yielded supremacy to the fear of making a mistake? Why is it now considered so much more embarrassing to be deceived by hope than by fear? One reason for Christianity becoming a world religion was the promise of hope it held out for all those (a very large majority in the ancient world) who did not have much to hope for in this life. Not that a successful churchman like St. Augustine (ignorant of modern science) was any less familiar with the intellectual "offense" of the Cross than a nineteenth-century agnostic ("lest it should believe falsehoods, it refused to be cured"), but Augustine, contrary to the latter, came to realize "that unless we should believe, we should do nothing at all in this life." In both instances there is a common condition of "hanging in suspense" and "being strangled," followed by a profound parting of the ways. The passion that led to Augustine's conversion has yielded its "supreme wisdom" to the autonomy of critical reason. Even converts to Marxism invoke science as their guide, let alone Christian Scientists.

The Fascists have their "scientific" theories of race and the followers of Norman Vincent Peale keep abreast of the latest scientific information on the normal personality Ours is still an age of scientific faiths. James would be little amused by this inner contradiction.

He carried on the Kantian revolution against empirical and rational dogmatism in metaphysics. Although Kant's own philosophy was limited by an excessive intellectualism that had its roots in the acceptance of Newtonian physics as normative, Kant nevertheless succeeded in showing that man's instinctive quest for rest or final answers can be squelched neither by the limitations of his critical understanding nor by the presumptuous claims of his reason to know where only surmise is possible. James, so to speak, existentialized Kant by extending the concept of regulative ideas to self-authenticating statements whose truth lies in the living and acting on them and whose falsity, conversely, emerges from their existential inadequacy for the individual. He even anticipated the view now associated with Sartre that human beings are often instrumental in creating their own values *ex nihilo.* He speaks of faith helping to create facts where (through it) our response to situations changes not only us but the very reality to which it was made. Memorable here are his existentialist depictions of a predicament in the Alps and of a railroad robbery:

> Suppose for example, that I am climbing in the Alps, and have had the ill luck to work myself into a position from which the only escape is by a terrible leap. Being without similar experience, I have no evidence of my ability to perform it successfully; but hope and confidence in myself make me sure that I shall not miss my aim; and nerve my feet to execute what without those subjective emotions would perhaps have been impossible. But suppose that, on the contrary, the emotions of fear and mistrust preponderate; or suppose that having just read the *Ethics of Belief,* I feel it would be sinful to act upon an assumption unverified by previous experience—why, then I shall hesitate so long that at last, exhausted and trembling, and launching myself in a moment of

despair, I miss my foothold and roll into the abyss. . . .[17]

A whole train of passengers (individually brave enough) will be looted by a few highwaymen, simply because the latter can count on one another, while each passenger fears that if he makes a movement of resistance, he will be shot before any one else backs him up. If we believed that the whole car-full would rise at once with us, we should each severally rise, and train-robbing would never be attempted. There are, then, cases where a fact cannot come at all unless a preliminary faith exists in its coming. *And where faith in a fact can help create the fact,* that would be an insane logic which would say that faith running ahead of scientific evidence is the "lowest kind of immorality" into which a thinking man can fall. Yet such is the logic by which our scientific absolutists pretend to regulate our lives.[18]

What matters most to James is not the vindication of a "rational faith" extrinsic to the realm of verifiable knowledge, but the legitimate place of overbeliefs in the context of human living. Although Kant elevates the practical reason, his stress remains on thought self-driven beyond the bounds of cognition. Instead, James emphasizes the exigencies of existence that demand risk-taking on nonverifiable grounds. For him it is not merely a question of mental unrest entitled to metaphysical solace, but of the whole person in danger of destroying himself by fence-straddling and erosive temporizing. Implicit in his argument for the "will to believe" is the fear of the inhumanity of men reduced to thinking machines who, presumably for the sake of accuracy, desist from revealing themselves by any "unnecessary" gesture, word, or passion.

In *The Varieties of Religious Experience* James openly declares his sympathy for the "twice-born" or neurotic personality, which he unfashionably preferred to "healthy-mindedness." A great deal of the book's fascination derives from its exploration of the more unusual phases of the religious life. "It always leads to a better understanding of a thing's significance to consider its exaggerations and perversions, its equivalents and substitutes and nearest relatives elsewhere." [19] This non-Aristotelian preoccupation with the twisted or extraordinary, as previously indicated, is a characteristic feature of existentialist reflection James was temperamentally drawn to the twilight manifestations of the human spirit. At the same time he acknowledged that the esoteric moments of the religious consciousness have their counterparts in the normal flow of events with which most of us are familiar. Thus he expresses a basic criticism of our civilization which Freud made commonplace:

> The normal process of life contains moments as bad as any of those which insane melancholy is filled with, moments in which radical evil gets its innings and takes its solid turn. The lunatic's visions of horror are all drawn from the material of daily fact. Our civilization is founded on the shambles, and every individual existence goes out in a lonely spasm of helpless agony. If you protest, my friend, wait till you arrive there yourself.[20]

The whole book is a protest against overintellectualism in modern thought in general and in religion in particular "The folly of the cross, so inexplicable by the intellect, has yet its indestructible vital meaning." [21] Unable to embrace anything like Dewey's "common faith" or related varieties of liberal enlightenment, James goes out of his empirical way to vindicate those irrational elements in man's spiritual life which the *philosophes* had proposed to banish.[22] It is the pretentiousness of the intellect in religion as anywhere else to claim self-sufficiency which James cannot accept:

> I need not discredit philosophy by laborious criticisms of its arguments. It will suffice if I show that as a matter of history it fails to prove its pretensions to be "objectively" convincing. In fact, philosophy does so fail. It does not banish differences; it founds schools and sects just as feeling does. I believe, in fact, that the logical reason of man operates in this field of divinity exactly as it has always operated in love, or in patriotism, or in politics, or in any other of the wider affairs of life, in which our passions, or our mystical intuitions fix our beliefs beforehand. It finds

arguments for our convictions, for indeed it has to find them. It amplifies and defines our faith, and signifies it and lends it words and plausibility. It hardly ever engenders it; it cannot now secure it.[23]

Characteristically he goes on to contrast "the interest of the individual in his private personal destiny" with the "impersonality of the scientific attitude utterly repudiating the personal point of view." [24] He finds the latter wanting in matters of ultimate concern to human beings without losing sight of the fact that "though a scientist may individually nourish a religion, and be a theist in his irresponsible hours, the days are over when it could be said that for Science herself the heavens declare the glory of God and the firmament showeth his handiwork." [25]

With regard to the value crisis in modern thought James occupies a position midway between Hume and Kierkegaard. Like Hume, James is an empiricist at heart, an advocate of scientific method, an enemy of obscure speculation, and an analyst of reason in the grips of sentiment. Like Kierkegaard, James is familiar with anxiety: he sees life as risky and precarious, he emphasizes the agony of decision and responsibility, he defends the individual against the implications of collectivism, and, most important, he repudiates scientific neutrality as a possible attitude for men to take on questions of human existence. Unlike Kierkegaard, James endorsed a Leap which never attained the fixed paradoxical tensions of Christological mystery, but a necessary Leap beyond the available evidence it was indeed. Unlike Hume, James did not have a placid temperament, and so could not even pretend to play billiards, waiting for God to become an analytic or synthetic proposition, but the philosophical difficulties involved he continued to face nevertheless. Had James come across *The Sickness unto Death* he would have discovered a surprising confirmation of his treatment of faith: religious truth, Kierkegaard shows us there, is not a matter of assenting to propositions, but of the self living with itself in hope rather than despair.

CHAPTER IV

The Breakdown of Autonomy:
Dostoevsky and the Sickness unto Death

The relation to himself a man cannot get rid of any more than he can get rid of himself, which moreover is one and the same thing, since the self is the relationship to oneself.

Søren Kierkegaard [1]

While William James, in striking contrast to Dewey, was not wholly insensitive to the atmosphere of crisis in the writings of such thinkers as Schopenhauer, Nietzsche, and Tolstoy, he refrained from spelling out the implications of his moral and religious philosophy in any comparable radical vein. As suggested earlier, this failure may be attributed to the "genteel tradition" and also, conceivably, to certain self-protective instincts. Nietzsche and Tolstoy virtually sacrificed themselves to their sense of honesty, just as Kierkegaard's dissent from Christendom entailed a tortured existence for this dialectical poet. Whatever the nature of James's limitations may have been, it is in spite of them that he succeeded in pushing the horizons of American philosophy to a point of contact with European trends of thought which, alas, has not since been duplicated or preserved.

James, in seeing man both as obligated and entitled to choose his own destiny, does not worry enough about the possible distortions of freedom. Individuals in the modern world are subject not only to enslavement by statistics and pseudo science, but, as in all times, to the tyranny of their own wills. It is because they cannot live with themselves that men often acquiesce in equivocation and fence-straddling. Granted that natural science is no final arbiter of human self-realization, does this make the individual inwardly free to seek his best advantage? Are not his darker moods as insistent on satisfaction as his (Jamesian) cravings for blessedness and immortality? James knew the threat to autonomy from the outside, but his liberal Protestant conscience did not reckon sufficiently with the inversions of humanism that will destroy the self from within. Kierkegaard and Dostoevsky in two brilliant independently conceived but congruent works provide the "will to believe" with this missing dimension of human perversity.

Since the Enlightenment ennui and despair have become dominant themes in Western literature. Scarcely a major work of fiction still views man's nature and destiny under the aspect of hope or fulfillment. Why this should be so is the subject of interminable discussion which, generally speaking, locates the deeper cause in the breakdown of virtually all genuine religiousness with an attendant rise in meaninglessness and emptiness. This development in turn is linked to the various revolutions, particularly the industrial, that have combined to undermine traditional Occidental modes of thought and living. While there is some disagreement whether it is merely a question of modern society becoming gradually accustomed to the blessings so precipitously conferred upon it by technology, thus comparing its present growing pains to those of an adolescent, few seem to disagree on the prevailing exhaustion and anxiety. In addition to the note of doom struck by the best minds of our day—and its currency is no sufficient argument against its truth—it would appear that the unreflecting masses quite apart from being exposed to this literature do not know how to redeem their leisure time, have lost a great deal of capacity for spontaneous participation in public affairs, and seek despairingly if not eagerly for something vital to which they can relate themselves and through which they will find renewed structure in their lives. Granted that characters in a novel by Dostoevsky, Melville, D. H. Lawrence, Kafka, Mann, or Camus are not a representative sample of "real" society, they still illuminate it better than the statistics of soci ologists describing a nonexistent average. Both Kierkegaard and Dostoevsky, whose analyses of modern despair remain prototypal, acknowledged a close connection between the imagination of the poet creating a unique instance of a phenomenon commonly observed and the condition of actual men, without, however, blurring the distinction implicit here: "It need hardly be said," writes Dostoevsky in the Preface of *Letters from the Underworld,*

> that both the writer of these "Letters" and the "Letters" themselves are creatures of the imagination. Nevertheless, in view of the circumstances under which, in general, our community has become formed, such men as the writer in question not only may, but are bound, to exist.[2]

And Kierkegaard voices a similar sentiment on this issue:

> Ah, demoniac madness! He rages most of all at the thought that eternity might get it into its head to take his misery from him! This sort of despair is seldom seen in the world, such figures generally are met with only in the works of poets, that is to say, of real poets, who always lend their characters this "demoniac" ideality (taking this word in the purely Greek sense). Nevertheless such a despairer is to be met with also in real life.[3]

Letters from the Underworld and *The Sickness unto Death* were written fifteen years apart (1864 and 1849 respectively) by authors who knew nothing of each other's existence and who moreover came from radically different backgrounds. What Kierkegaard, the disillusioned Lutheran in Christendom, and Dostoevsky, the persecuted Russian nationalist in Czardom, had in common was a remarkable sensitivity to the signs of their times as well as uncanny insight into the hearts and minds of men. Not only were they both psychological geniuses, but each in his way set out to reaffirm the passion of a Christian faith (however heterodox) as a corrective to competing ideologies of the nineteenth century. On first acquaintance they are predominantly negative thinkers, always inclined to attack and tear down even that—such as Romanticism—to which they are personally drawn. Yet the full force of their destructive criticism would be missed if dissociated from its dialectical counterpart: a sustained conviction that man's greatest problem everywhere and any time is to be properly related to himself and that this relationship can only be sound if ultimately anchored in the presence of God. To be sure, Dostoevsky and Kierkegaard never espoused the same kind of Christianity. Nor, by any means, were they untouched by the irreligious doubts and anxieties that bothered their contemporaries.[4] Indeed, in terms of a strict ecclesiastical measure it is arguable that they were not Christian thinkers at all. The point is that together they viewed the human situation as a predicament rooted in its alienation from a higher Power. Their shared political conservatism, their contempt for middle-class acquiescence in philistinism, their suspiciousness of secular utopianism, their preoccupation with love and suffering as soteriological values are worthy of note, though secondary in import to their conviction of man's fall from a state of grace which he cannot regain by himself alone. On their view the dimensions of the heavenly and the hellish are inseparable from the other dimensions in which humanity strives for transcendence.

The narrator of *Letters from the Underworld* has become a familiar character in modern literature. Sick, disgusted, intelligent, understanding and yet not understanding; seeking redemption in the lowest depths of being, he embodies the spirit of Mephistopheles reduced to unheroic proportions or of the Vicomte de Valmont, the hero-villain in Laclos's *Les Liaisons dangereuses*, reincarnated in nineteenth-century St. Petersburg. His story is simple. Burdened by heredity with antisocial instincts, orphaned at an early age, and raised in a tyrannical school environment, he has come to hate everyone and everything, not least of all himself. He sees himself as a bundle of resentments ready to take offense at the slightest provocation and even where such grounds are entirely lacking.[5] When he does not feel insulted he broods, and when not brooding plunges into an orgy of activity in order to escape boredom. What he thinks he wants most of all is peace and quiet, but no sooner are these states of mind realizable possibilities than he goes out of his way to see to it that they do not become actualities. While sharing with the heroes of Romantic literature a calculating prudence superimposed on a wounded heart, he is too perceptive to get wrapped up in their daydreams unless it be to indulge in reveries of emulating Napoleon. Unlike Julien Sorel, for example, he is not interested in making his way in the world at all costs, for he has already despaired of what the world calls success, and hence gone underground. In this respect he has prophetic affinities with Kafka's tortured souls. Yet for all his hatred of visible reality and existence his dissatisfaction with these is far from final. Periodically he finds it desirable to emerge from his soured state and resume traffic with society. Interestingly enough, the underworldly monasticism of his kind in modern fiction is rarely consistent. Each Walden Pond must have its Concord close by, if only to set it in sharp relief. The Underground Man, like so many seekers of solitude, perennially craves for an antithesis to snarl at with clenched teeth. What he professes to despise makes his escape from it inversely heroic.

In addition to his reflections on the moral bankruptcy of nineteenth-century men with hypersensitive souls and his longing for "the great and the beautiful," he focuses his narrative on two personal encounters that apparently meant a great deal to him. One was being insulted by an officer whom he paid back handsomely, devoting an inordinate amount of time and energy to his sweet revenge. The other was a visit to a brothel following a dinner with his former school-fellows, where not altogether without cause he felt himself horribly abused by the company and proceeded to spoil the party so far as that lay within his power, the festivities having reduced themselves to a drunken brawl *à l'ancienne Russe*. It is during this episode that he meets Liza, whom he commences to lecture—no doubt under the influence of Fichte—on the sins of the flesh and the dignity of the married state. This meeting with a second "fallen" person is a typically Dostoevskyan situation save that in this instance it does not lead to mutual redemption. Liza responds to the Underground Man's entreaties to change her profession by accepting his invitation to visit him at home. (Much to his regret, in retrospect, he had given her his address.) Instead of welcoming her as the instrument of his salvation from despair and self-torment or just being civil, he treats her with icy contempt. For a time he does not address a single word to her, realizing of course that for Liza this unnatural silence is tantamount to a living death. She intuits his great unhappiness and for a moment, which he passionately seizes in a fit of physical desire, yields herself to him in order, so she hopes, to bring him around to himself. But to no avail! So deeply ingrained is his self-hatred that he must destroy the very possibility of losing his chains. Even self-sacrificing Liza, who knows the experience of prostitution, can no longer put up with his treatment of her. He wants her to return right after she has run down the stairs, though he is still clear-sighted enough to admit to himself that it would be the same thing all over again. Nowhere in modern literature is the split between excitement and feeling better delineated.

Above all, the Underground Man prizes his freedom. And by it he means little more than being able to do as he pleases. There is a beguiling mixture of truth and error in his attack on the diversified cult of scientific determinism in nineteenth-century thought. It need only be recalled here that Marxists, Darwinians, Benthamites, Saint-Simonians, and their numerous disciples of the goddess Science all labored under the illusion that their excursions into the philosophy of man were strict *Wissenschaft*. Or, if they did not go quite so far, they held that in principle, at any rate, science could and should be the norm for human values. The Underground Man, quite correctly in this case, resents the progressive "dehumanization" of individuals into "piano-keys." [6] Dostoevsky and Kierkegaard would agree with him that to obscure individual responsibility and freedom in a maze of bad metaphysics, pretentious statistics, and pseudo-scientific speculation (all unrelated to concrete forms of human existence) is pernicious for human welfare. They would support his critique of utilitarian utopianism and its naïve faith in the redeeming power of civilization. Today such criticism is commonplace, but in 1864 it was highly unorthodox and it is far from ineffectively voiced even for us:

Advantage, indeed? What, after all, *is* advantage? Would *you*, gentlemen, undertake exactly to define wherein human advantage consists? What if human advantage not only *may*, but *does*, consist of the fact that, on certain occasions, man may desire, not what is good for him, but what is bad? . . . Can human interests *ever be* properly reckoned up? May there not always remain interests which never have been, never can be, included in any classification? . . . May there not, therefore, exist something which to most men is even dearer than their true interests? Or, not to infringe the logical sequence, may there not exist some supreme interest of interests (the additional interest of which I am speaking) which is greater and more absorbing than any other interest, and for which man, if the need should arise, is ready to contravene every law, and to lose sight alike of common sense, honor, prosperity and ease—in a word, of all the things which are fair and expedient—if haply he can gain for himself that primal, that supreme, advantage which he conceives to be the dearest thing on earth? [7]

The Underground Man would not have been so naïve as to apprehend the totalitarianism of a Hitler as a return to precivilized barbarism:

Civilization develops in man nothing but an added capacity for receiving impressions. That is all. And the growth of that capacity further augments man's tendency to seek pleasure in blood-letting. . . . Possibly you may say that all this happened in a comparatively barbarous age—that even at the present day the times are barbarous—that golden pins are still being thrust into people's breasts—that though man in many things, has learnt to see clearer now than he used to do in *more* barbarous ages, he has not yet learnt to act wholly as reason and science would have him do. Yet all the while, I know, you are persuaded in your own minds that man is bound to improve as soon as ever he has dropped some old, bad customs of his, and allowed science and healthy thought alone to nourish, to act as the normal directors of human nature. Yet, I know that you are persuaded that eventually man will cease to err *of set purpose*, or to let his will clash with his normal interests. On the contrary (say you), science will in time show man (though, in your opinion, it is superfluous to do so) that he does not possess *any* will or initiative of his own, and never has done, but that he is as the keyboard of a piano, or as the handle of a hurdy-gurdy.[8]

In stressing man's love for adversity and destruction as being as much a part of his makeup as his desire for order and prosperity, he offers a realistic appraisal of the threats and ambiguities that inhere in every mode of existence. "Reason is an excellent thing—I do not deny that for a moment; but reason is reason, and no more, and satisfies only the reasoning faculty in man, whereas volition is a manifestation of all life (that is to say, human life as a whole, with reason and every other sort of appendage included)." [9]

But Dostoevsky and Kierkegaard would emphatically take issue with the Underground Man's conception of freedom. It is his tragedy, so to speak, that while being felicitous in the construction of definitions—"man is a creature which walks on two legs and is devoid of gratitude"—and in his grasp of abstract questions, he is unsuccessful in dealing with himself. In Kierkegaard's terminology, he cannot transmute ideal possibilities into existential realities, a process that contrary to the Hegelian dialectic does not proceed in and of itself. Even where he existentially duplicates his notion of freedom, in practice it turns out to be self-contradictory and illusory. He becomes a prisoner of his own passions and capricious impulses. "Without a pure heart there can be no full, no true, realization of self," he declaims,[10] but if a man be without a pure heart—as he himself admits being—how can he possibly rely on himself for the sole authority of his conduct? By setting himself up as his own deity he cuts himself off from any outside influence that might give his freedom some foil and thus some meaning. Revolutionary political parties from the Jacobins to the Communists have made the same mistake. Obsessed with being the Opposition,[11] they could only define themselves creatively in terms of resentment. As soon as they came to power and had to act responsibly they fell into daemonic idolatry. The fate of the Underground Man is a singular version, prophetic as so many of Dostoevsky's constructions, of the "kingdom of heaven on earth" that "idealists" left and right have been promising to establish since 1789.

The Sickness unto Death traces a few key directions despair takes in the lives of men. Ordinarily the term is used to describe a state of disenchantment with things in general or with oneself brought on by a nervous breakdown, frustrated hope, irreparable loss, or some other calamity in experience. For Kierkegaard this is the despair of immediacy, a comparatively mild case of the sickness, since the individual affected by it need not have any understanding of his condition and will in all likelihood be predisposed to locate its cause outside himself. Despair would not be the sickness unto death if it responded to a change of air, mood, environment, or psychoanalyst. Ultimately every form of despair from that endured by neglected maidens at a dance to Satan's in hell is tied to the sickness, although Kierkegaard focuses on those manifestations that presuppose a considerable degree of self-reflection and awareness. Hence most aspects under which he examines despair are particularly germane to the feverishly conscious Underground Man. As the sickness unto death despair refers fundamentally to a self that has despaired over itself so that in weakness or defiance it remains divided—the individual cannot bear to be and face himself as himself. To do so, in despair and always short of a real cure, he adopts poses and stratagems which, temporarily, conceal his self from himself and give him the illusion of not being a self or being a "new" self. Eccentrics who periodically become Napoleon or Balzac exemplify obtrusively, but not necessarily at great intensity, a common human trait of desiring to get rid of oneself and be somebody else or, like the Underground Man, to become an "insect" instead of a man.[12]

Just as the Underground Man vacillates constantly between periods of extreme self-degradation and unconfined self-esteem, so Kierkegaard opposed any view of the self which regards it either as entirely autonomous or as totally insignificant. For him the claim of the eternal upon it makes it at once infinitely precious as well as infinitely dependent. Thus despair can be equally the result of illusions of grandeur consciously or unconsciously entertained as of fits of hatred for oneself and the whole of existence. The individual who has altogether soured on life is as sick as the familiar middle-aged lady who "loves" everything—Mohammed, Van Gogh's sunflowers, and Nietzsche's Zarathustra poems thrown into her infinite capacity for being transfixed. Christianity's stand on the joint dignity and misery of man before God underlies Kierkegaard's notion of what a self ought to become if it is not to linger in despair. It must have faith—by virtue of the absurd perhaps—that for God all things are possible while it is impossible for the individual self to be God. The center of the self is its divine eternal source. Once that is lost sight of or denied, it is doomed to squander itself in the realms of the fantastic-beautiful and the fantastic-ugly. Faith is a dead option for the Underground Man. He cannot even believe in Liza, let alone in the invisible God of theism. It is in terms of the negative theology, of Godforsakenness and rebellion, that he bears witness to the nothingness of man without God. Here again the author of the "Grand Inquisitor" and the author of *The Sickness unto Death* and *Training in Christianity* struck a most prophetic note: For modern Western man it often seems that the only conditions under which religion can be existentially illuminating are those of absurdity where religion is existentially denied. Goethe's Faust, Dostoevsky's Underground Man, Melville's Captain Ahab, Kierkegaard's

Seducer, Kafka's K.—these, not the insipid moralizers of so-called religious fiction, testify to the glory of God, even in hell.

Much to the horror of some professional philosophers and new critics of literature, the coupling of Dostoevsky and Kierkegaard has already done irremediable harm, especially where the philosophers do not regard Christian thought as verifiable or analytic, and where the literary critics discover an ominous lack of symbolism in novels of ideas. Under these circumstances the close affinity between the Underground Man's despair and the aspects under which Kierkegaard examines it in *The Sickness unto Death* might well irritate both camps still further. If the argument here reveals an incongruous relationship between a work of imagination and a work of thought this is so much the worse for the "age of analysis." *Letters from the Underworld* requires philosophical (in the broadest sense of the word) explication to become fully intelligible not only as a significant document in the history of ideas but also as a literary and psychological milestone in autobiography:

> I wish, in particular, to try whether one can *ever* be really open with oneself—*ever* be really fearless of any item of truth. *En passant*, Heine has said that a true autobiography is practically impossible, since every man lies to himself. In his (Heine's) opinion, even Rousseau, in his *Confessions*, lied—partly out of set purpose, and partly out of vanity. And I believe that Heine is right. I myself know how vanity may lead a man to impute whole crimes to himself; of the working of such vanity I have a good idea. But Heine was speaking of men who write their confessions for the public eye, whereas I wish to write but for myself alone. . . . Moreover, I do not wish to be restricted in the scope of my writing. Consequently I intend to observe therein no order or system. What I remember, that I shall write down.[13]

The Underground Man is no professor of anything except suffering. But being fairly well-educated and read he cannot help pouring out his soul—as no one in Western literature had poured it out before him—he cannot help sharing with the reader his reflections on his experience. Taking a work written in 1849 as a commentary on another composed fifteen years later constitutes an inversion of natural sequence, but *The Sickness unto Death* happens to be the best and only worthy companion to *Letters from the Underworld*. What cries out for interpretation in Dostoevsky's narrative is clarified and sharpened by Kierkegaard's brilliant exposition. Both with respect to contents and language this is one of the great inadvertent marriages of minds in modern intellectual history.[14]

The Universality of This Sickness (Despair)

So far as I am concerned, I have but carried to a finish in my life, what you have never even dared to carry half-way, although you have constantly mistaken your cowardice for prudence, you have constantly cheated yourself with comforting reflections. The truth is that I have been more alive than you. •

There lives not one single man after all who is not to some extent in despair, in whose inmost parts there does not dwell a disquietude, a perturbation, a discord, an anxious dread of an unknown something, or of something he does not even dare to make acquaintance with, dread of a possibility of life, or dread of himself, so that, after all, as physicians speak of a man going about with a disease in him, this man is going about and carrying a sickness of the spirit, which only rarely and in glimpses, by and with a dread which to him is inexplicable, gives evidence of its presence within.••

Towards the end of his confession the Underground Man challenges his abstract judges—whom he addresses as "gentlemen"—to make good on their righteousness over against him and by extension to all the other "down and out" in the world. He does not have a *moral* leg to

• *Letters from the Underworld*, p. 149.
•• *The Sickness unto Death*, p. 155.

stand on in thus comparing himself to his fellow men; still Kierkegaard would agree with his implicit affirmation of universal despair. One of the most ironic features of the argument in *The Sickness unto Death*—a feature pointing ahead to psychoanalytic theory—is the claim that however contrary the appearances, something of despair lurks beneath them. Moreover, some of the least eradicable forms of the sickness are precisely those of which no cognizance is taken. The hiddenness of despair[15] is an important aspect of its universality. For Kierkegaard this despairing condition of mankind can in large measure be attributed to its inordinate attachment to things earthly and transient. If the significance of life for an individual is centered in contingency—as it is for the majority—then the threat of nonbeing is his constant companion. Existentialist writers have often been taken to task for overemphasizing despair and its related moods at the expense of joy. Apart from the historical reasons for this being the case (Western civilization has not exactly engendered a spirit of hope during the past century), in Kierkegaard there is the characteristic Christian mistrust of worldliness. In the most ecstatic moments of human life—childbirth, love, revelation—a note of dread is never far behind. The miraculousness of a supreme work of art is its momentary conquest of anxiety. So it might be said that the Underground Man has had his eyes opened to the daemonic potential not only in himself but in the world at large. He has been more alive than his contemporaries by virtue of courting the abyss on which all life hangs suspended.

The Hiddenness of This Sickness (*Despair*)

> Every day I keep discovering in myself elements of the most opposite order conceivable, and can feel them swarming within me, and am aware that, to the very end of my life, they will continue so to swarm. Yet, often as they have striven to manifest themselves outwardly, I have never allowed them to do so. •

• *Letters from the Underworld*, p. 7.

Not only that he who suffers [despair] may wish to hide from it and may be able to do so, to the effect that it can so dwell in a man that no one, no one whatever discovers it; no, rather that it can be so hidden in a man that he himself does not know it. •

As suggested above, the universality of despair is correlated with its hiddenness. On a vulgar view it would appear ridiculous to maintain that everyone is in despair when so many individuals not only act cheerfully but are convinced of their high spirits. Yet it is Kierkegaard's belief, also borne out by some acquaintance with human character, that what a man essentially is cannot be inferred from how he conducts himself in society. Nor, as is common knowledge today, is an individual's opinion of himself any less suspect at face value. In fact, Kierkegaard proceeds to argue that the milder forms of despair are the transparent kind, which is not to say that they should not be taken seriously. But just as the earnest potential suicide will talk little about his act ahead of time, so the individual deeply affected by despair is not apt to parade his condition in front of everyone. Part of his sickness is being locked up within himself, a prisoner of his own passions and thoughts. He may go out of his way to conceal his unhappiness, if not successfully from himself then at least from others. The unnatural animation with which many people talk—trying to seem sincere—is indicative of such a move, though here the concealment breaks down. In severer cases it is frequently remarked that so-and-so is simply impenetrable, the observer suspecting that something is amiss in spite of the even-tempered and genial deportment of the observed. The Underground Man attempts to get through the chores of the day without disclosing his actual state of mind. Possibly because he does this with so much deliberation and pride (self-centeredness) his pose is a failure. From his own account his contemporaries would not have mistaken him for a happy man. Liza alone saw lovingly and clearly into his wretchedness. Significantly enough he

• *The Sickness unto Death,* p. 160.

could not even confide in her, for to confide is an attempt to share the relationship with oneself with someone else. This a despairer often cannot do.[16] Those who shrink from the idea of the hiddenness of despair are apt to be the same people who insist that all extroverts are happy and all introverts maladjusted.

The Sickness unto Death Is Despair

> I wish to tell you gentlemen (no matter whether you care to hear it or not), why I have never been able to become an insect. I solemnly declare to you that I have often *wished* to become an insect, but never could attain my desire. I swear to you, gentlemen, that to be overcharged with sensibility is an actual malady—a real, a grievous malady. For humanity's daily need mere ordinary human sensibility ought to suffice, or about one-half or one quarter of the sensibility which falls to the lot of the average educated man of our miserable nineteenth century. . . . ●

> The possibility of this sickness is man's advantage over the beasts; to be sharply observant of this sickness constitutes the Christian's advantage over the natural man; to be healed of this sickness is the Christian's bliss.●●

There is something dialectically proper about the Underground Man's desire to become an insect. For an insect has this advantage over a man: it cannot fall into despair.[17] Kierkegaard views the sickness unto death both as an advantage and a drawback, both as a sickness and a cure, both as man's unique opportunity and his terrible temptation. "Ethically-religiously" speaking, to fall into despair can have the most serious consequences for the individual when, like the Underground Man, he succumbs to nihilism in reflection as well as in deed. Also, to despair of God and forgiveness of sins has consistently been recognized as the greatest sin. On the other hand, it is the

● *Letters from the Underworld,* p. 9.
●● *The Sickness unto Death,* p. 24.

possibility of falling into despair, of feeling the claim of the eternal upon oneself, that helps to distinguish man from lesser rational and nonspiritual creatures. The Romantic longing for what was thought of as the simple happiness of savages, particularly relating to sex, and the bourgeois materialism of the French *philosophes* and their disciples are of the same vintage, according to which mere self-satisfaction and repose would constitute the *summum bonum*. Implicit no less in the daydreaming of the Romantic as in the crudeness of the materialist is a denial of man's spiritual nature.

> For not to be in despair may mean to be in despair, and it may also mean to be delivered from being in despair. A sense of security and tranquility may mean that one is in despair, precisely this security, this tranquility, may be despair; and it may mean that one has overcome despair and gained peace. . . . It is not true of despair, as it is of bodily sickness, that the feeling of indisposition is the sickness. By no means. The feeling of indisposition is again dialectical. Never to have been sensible of this indisposition is precisely to be in despair.[18]

The initial restive disposition of Romantic writers was one of their healthier features. Never to have become aware of oneself as a spiritual being inadequate in the sight of a higher power which requires it to become a self may be indigenous to Tahitian manhood, but its truthfulness as a mode of existence is far less self-evident than its attractiveness. The Underground Man with all his liabilities must be given credit for his willingness to seek himself and "the good and the beautiful" above and beyond convention, respectability, and surface smoothness. Herein he resembles the Romantic hero: always adrift and when in port forlorn. The dialectic of the Romantic quest, whereby it is at once pernicious and salutary, is this: the self is sensibly dissatisfied with itself as wanting in something, but it lacks the necessary determinants to find itself, and as a result loses itself still further in fantastic visions and irrelevant possibilities.

Kierkegaard's position on the dialectical advantages of

despair as opposed to its ethical-religious dangers has given rise to numerous misunderstandings. He is not saying that any form of suffering is unambiguously good; at the same time he could not maintain with Bernard Shaw that poverty, for example, is necessarily evil. Human beings respond redemptively, sometimes to adversity, on other occasions to well-being. And no one can tell in advance about this matter, least of all the person directly concerned. Despair, respectable opinion would have it, is bad, just like chicken pox. For one thing, it disturbs the self, for another, the world prefers a smiling countenance to a sourpuss. No wonder Flaubert choked with rage on beholding his French brethren whose outlook on things was of course perfectly normal. For the Underground Man to want to be an insect is an attempt to evade the responsibility that has been thrust upon him by virtue of his humanity. His quest for self-knowledge fails not because he despaired over himself and existence, but because he defiantly refused help out of this despair. Nevertheless, the wanderings of his heightened sensibility, in spite of himself, place him closer to God than any lily in the field. For man, which is the point of the New Testament parable, can only *become* like a lily in the field while the lily *is* what it is by nature. When despair impels a man to become aware of himself as a self for the first time, when it is instrumental in denting his spiritlessness and waking him from his vegetative slumbers, it is good. This does not contradict Kierkegaard's correlative notion that to remain in despair is the height of sin.[19]

Despair Viewed under the Aspect Possibility/Necessity

Does a wall, forsooth, constitute a full-stop, a signal for the cessation of the struggle, for the mere reason that it and the formula that twice two make four are one? Oh, blindness of blindness! What, rather, we should all do is to comprehend everything, to envisage everything—to comprehend and to envisage every impossibility and every stone wall; to accept no single impossibility, no single stone wall, if we do not feel inclined to accept it; to attain (in spite of the most inevitable combinations and the most re-futative conclusions of logic) to the eternal truth that one may be at fault even in regard to a stone wall, no matter how much one may *seem* not to be at fault; lastly, (in recognizing that fact, to subside silently, and with lips compressed to resignation, and with a bittersweet feeling in one's heart, into a state of inertia. •

If one will compare the tendency to run wild in possibility with the efforts of a child to enunciate words, the lack of possibility is like being dumb. Possibility becomes more and more intense—but only in the sense of possibility, not in the sense of actuality; for in the sense of actuality the meaning of intensity is that at least something of that which is possible becomes actual. At the instant something appears possible, and then a new possibility makes its appearance, at last this phantasmagoria moves so rapidly that it is as if everything were possible—and this is precisely the last moment, when the individual becomes for himself a mirage. . . . Necessity is like a sequence of consonants only, but in order to utter them there must in addition be possibility. When this is lacking, when a human existence is brought to pass that it lacks possibility, it is in despair, and every instant it lacks possibility it is in despair.••

The Underground Man embodies in an extreme form a distinguishing characteristic of humanity: namely, the desire for what is unattainable. He is obsessed by the pursuit of the impossible, which for him means freedom. He rants against every supposed obstacle to the satis-faction of his will. At one moment he acknowledges no "impossibility," at the next he subsides "into a state of inertia," "with a bittersweet feeling in [his] heart." As, according to Kierkegaard, "the lack of infinitude means to be desperately narrow-minded and mean-spirited," the lack of finitude "is the powerlessness to obey, to submit to the necessary in oneself, to what may be called one's limit." [20] Once more the Underground Man vacillates

• *Letters from the Underworld*, p. 17.
•• *The Sickness unto Death*, pp. 169-71.

between these two extremes. His Romanticism enables him to rise above the drudgery of common sense while his materialism should keep him in good stead with actuality. But being in despair (unrelated to himself) he cannot even take advantage of his virtues, which together with his shortcomings, come to function as instruments of self-destruction. His reflective imagination becomes fantastical—"the self becomes a sort of abstract sentimentality which is so inhuman that it does not apply to any person, but inhumanly participates feelingly, so to speak, in the fate of one or another abstraction, e.g., that of mankind in *abstracto;* the more knowledge increases, the more it becomes a kind of inhuman knowing for the production of which man's self is squandered." [21] And his shrewdness instead of easing his path through the pitfalls of worldliness degenerates into a calculating malice that must end in bitter resignation and disillusionment. To pursue a bit further the Romantic/Materialist dichotomy that circumscribes the Underground Man's abortive search for freedom: while the Romantics (F. Schlegel in *Lucinde,* Byron in *Childe Harold,* and Constant in *Adolphe*) were predisposed to dispense with all conventionality and restraint, the dialecticians (Hegel by his categories of man as citizen or as victim, Engels-Marx by their category of the class) reduced individual human existence to a level of virtual meaninglessness. In one case the self vaporizes itself into disconnected moments of euphoria and depression, in the other it becomes completely subordinated to impersonal forces such as the "logic of history." In the Lutheran sense we are truly free only by being redemptively bound. This means that the expression of individuality derives its ultimate sanction from the grace of God, by which it is freed not from sin but from its persistence in sin—the Underground Man's self-torment.

Despair Viewed under the Aspect of Consciousness

I am extremely self-conscious. •

With every increase in the degree of consciousness,

• *Letters from the Underworld,* p. 11.

and in proportion to that increase, the intensity of despair increases: the more consciousness, the more intense the despair. . . . The devil's despair is the most intense . . . for there is no obscurity which might serve as a mitigating excuse, his despair is therefore absolute defiance. •

"I am extremely self-conscious," remarks the Underground Man with a genius for understatement which belies his Russian origins. Like Hamlet he often bemoans his inability to act and compares himself unfavorably with those of lesser sensibility for whom stone walls do not exist. In fact, he regards self-consciousness as his sickness and suggests that the whole nineteenth century has succumbed to the same malady. True enough, Romanticism and German idealism had attached unprecedented significance to self-consciousness, under whose spell can be found together radical revolutionaries, Protestant pietists, adorers of nature, neomedievalists, and dreamers of every description. To be extremely conscious of things and of oneself is to be alive, and in spite of what might be said against the diverse utopian movements in the nineteenth-century thought, it cannot be denied that their founders and adherents had a tremendous capacity for responding to all sorts of experience. Being conscious, civilized, and alert in one's activity would seem to go hand in hand. But self-consciousness in particular, as Hamlet classically described it, can also have debilitating effects. By virtue of thinking much about himself the individual becomes more and more divorced from external reality. He starts to muse and brood over himself; before long he enters into monologues with himself and comes to resent any interruption as unwarranted, embarrassing, and terribly difficult to bear. Soon his egocentricity may make him unfit to live with—and worse, to live with himself. While recognizing a heightening of self-consciousness as a sign of spiritual awakening, Kierkegaard views it simultaneously as bringing about an increase in despair. For the highly self-conscious individual, if nothing else, comes to realize that the cause of his difficulty lies within

• *The Sickness unto Death,* p. 175.

himself. He is at once less deluded and less contented than the man of straight action. Just as beginning students of philosophy wonder why they should examine themselves and various views of the good life when not having thought about these matters before made them feel ignorantly happy, so persons of extreme self-consciousness lose a great deal of innocence and immediacy in exchange for an uncertain understanding of themselves. Hamlet's and the Underground Man's self-consciousness are equally dialectical: without it both would undoubtedly have been more socially acceptable, but without being themselves—pioneers in the life of the spirit. That Hamlet was "saved" and the Underground Man "damned" is another matter.

Despair over the Earthly or over Something Earthly

> Foam though I might at the mouth, I needed but to be given a doll to play with, or a cup of sweet tea to drink, and at once I sank to quiescence. •

> But dead he is not; there is, if you will, life in the characterization. In case everything suddenly changes, everything in the outward circumstances, and the wish is fulfilled, then life enters into him again, immediacy rises again, and he begins to live as fit as a fiddle. ••

This form of despair is the best-known and the most easily cured. Everyone, in diverse ways and degrees, to be sure, is upset by frustration, sometimes to the point of madness. The cries of the infant for some change in his environment, the sudden tears of childhood, the *Weltschmerz* of the adolescent, the disillusionment of the middle-aged, and the nagging bitterness of old age—all these are more or less normal manifestations of man not feeling at home in the world and not liking the fact. Although of little intensity in comparison to the Underground Man's *despair over himself and the forgiveness of his sins*, it is worth noting that his advance in self-consciousness and therefore in potentiated despair did not free him from the lighter

• *Letters from the Underworld,* p. 6.
•• *The Sickness unto Death,* p. 185.

forms of his sickness. Alas! the man who weeps over the loss of his razor blades will continue to weep over the loss of his razor blades even when weeping over himself. Like an avalanche the course of despair is accumulative. According to Kierkegaard, the individual in having passed through one stage, far from being done with it forever, will have to suffer it with the rest of his ailment.[22] "Every actual instant of despair is to be referred back to possibility, every instant the man in despair is contracting it, it is constantly in the present tense, nothing comes to pass here as a consequence of bygone actuality superseded; at every actual instant of despair the despairer bears as his responsibility all the foregoing experience in possibility as a present."[23] Even on a vulgar view it is comic to observe how individuals, having survived a great disaster, let us suppose, and having sworn never to get excited about trivialities again, resume doing so as soon as the normal swing of things is re-established. Most dedicated scholars, monks, and reformers, however hardworking, pious, and zealous they may actually be, are not entirely satisfied with their way of life. Here is further evidence for the universality of despair. The Underground Man, notwithstanding his contempt for society, must periodically re-enter it "to be given a doll to play with, or a cup of sweet tea to drink."

Despair about the Eternal or over Oneself

I was led by my boundless vanity and pretentiousness to look upon myself with a dissatisfaction that, at times, amounted almost to loathing. . . . Worse still, I would take it into my head that my countenance looked positively stupid, and feel overwhelmed with despair. At home I read a great deal, in a vain endeavor to drown in a flood of external impressions what was seething within me. Yet at times I grew terribly weary of it all and felt, that, come what might, I must embark upon some kind of activity. Hence I would suddenly plunge into the lowest depths of foul, dark—well, not so much debauchery, as lewdness, for at that time my passions were keen, and derived all the greater heat from the aching, perpetual discontent with the world of which I was full. . . . Above all things, constant depression seethed within me, a depression which, causing me to thirst for something different, for some sharp contrast, plunged me into vice. •

If there does not occur a radical change in the despairer so that he gets on the right path to faith, then such despair (the despair of introversion) will either potentiate itself to a higher form and continue to be introversion, or it breaks through to the outside and demolishes the outward disguise under which the despairing man has been living in his incognito. In the latter case such a despairer will then plunge into life, perhaps into the distractions of great undertakings, he will become a restless spirit which leaves only too clear a trace of its actual presence, a restless spirit which wants to forget, and inasmuch as the noise within is so loud stronger means are needed, though of a different sort, from those which Richard III employs in order not to hear his mother's curses. Or he will seek forgetfulness in sensuality, perhaps debauchery, in desperation he wants to return to immediacy, but constantly with the consciousness of the self, which he does not want to have. . . . ••

If the sickness unto death began and ceased with despair over the earthly or over something earthly it would be both less severe and more dangerous to the despairer; the former, because then reconciliation grounded in the flux of things would always have a higher degree of probability, and the latter, because the self in its attempt to evade the claim of the eternal upon itself merely postpones the issue by stubbornly persisting in childishness. Only children and idiots have legitimate cause not to despair of themselves. As for the rest of humanity, this is either a pose enchantingly displayed or a deliberate device to cultivate false innocence. Some time between

• *Letters from the Underworld,* pp. 50-5.
•• *The Sickness unto Death,* p. 199.

the ages of fourteen and twenty-one it should dawn on the loser of razor blades that his attitude towards the loss has as much to do with his resulting unhappiness as the loss itself. For the more serious questions of life this recognition is a milestone in spiritual growth.

Like the puritanically bred young girl away from home at her first fraternity party who goes off in a corner all by herself (so that *de facto* the party has ceased to exist for her) or plunges recklessly into the fun (so as to make up for her dour youth), the despairer in introspective despair has a choice between abandoning himself frantically to outside distractions or withdrawing still further into his shell. For the Underground Man a so-called higher pleasure, reading, initially presented the former possibility, but not for long: "hence I would suddenly plunge into the lowest depths of foul, dark—well, not so much debauchery, as lewdness. . . ." To follow Kierkegaard's analysis here: no radical change has occurred in the Underground Man's relationship to himself, consequently every activity he undertakes merely serves to cover up his affliction as eventually he yields to the morphine of sensual enticement. Having despaired over himself he cannot take refuge in blaming the world for his condition. The hostile attitude of many Christian writers, including Kierkegaard, to cultural activity as a substitute for faith may be said to rest on the Underground Man's confusion between reading as a delightful respite from the cares of daily living and as an answer to man's "metaphysical dread." As the beautiful sunset is succeeded, if not by an earthquake, then by a dull evening, so all aesthetic experience is subject to evaporation or decline. And what then with the agonized self that made it its "ultimate concern"? Corresponding exactly to Kierkegaard's account, the Underground Man "will seek forgetfulness in sensuality, perhaps in debauchery, in desperation he wants to return to immediacy, but constantly with the consciousness of the self, which he does not want to have."

The Despair of Willing Despairingly to be Oneself—Defiance

Occasionally repentance would seize me, but I always drove it forth again, for I was too weary to do aught but fall in with—rather, put up with—whatsoever chanced to happen. Yet all the while there was a way of escape which reconciled me to everything—namely the way of escape contained in my visionary cult of the "great and the beautiful." I did nothing but dream and dream of it; for three whole months on end I, crouching in my den, did nothing else. . . . That is to say, I had a sort of blind belief that one day some miracle, some external circumstance, would suddenly cause the present to break and become widened, and that suddenly there would dawn upon me a horizon of congenial, productive, fair, and above all things, *instant* activity (though in what manner instant I did not know), and that at last I should issue into God's world, mounted on a white horse, and crowned with laurels. . . . In those visions I would rise superior to all mankind; all men were in the dust before me, and forced to recognize my perfection as I extended to them my pardon. Yet I had not spent more than three months upon these ecstasies of mine when I began to feel a renewed inclination for intercourse with my fellow-men. . . . •

If the despairing self is active, it is related to itself only as experimenting with whatever it be that it undertakes, however great it may be, however astonishing, however persistently carried out. It acknowledges no power over it, hence in the last resort it lacks seriousness and is able to conjure up only a show of seriousness when the self bestows upon its experiments its utmost attention. Like the fire which Prometheus stole from the gods, so does this mean to steal from God the thought which is seriousness, that God is regarding one, instead of which the despairing self is content with regarding itself, and by that it is supposed to bestow upon its undertakings infinite interest and importance, whereas it is precisely this

• *Letters from the Underworld*, pp. 64-7.

which makes them mere experiments. For though this self were to go so far in despair that it becomes an "experimental god," no derived self can by regarding itself give itself more than it is: it nevertheless remains from first to last the self, by self-duplication it becomes neither more nor less than the self. The self is its own master, so it is said, absolutely its own lord, and precisely this is despair, but it also is what it regards as its pleasure and enjoyment. . . . The self wants to enjoy the entire satisfaction of making itself into itself, of developing itself, of being itself; it wants to have the honor of this poetical, this masterly plan according to which it has understood itself. And yet in the last resort it is a riddle how it understands itself; just at the *instant* when it seems to be nearest to having the fabric finished it can arbitrarily resolve the whole thing into nothing. •

Once again, these passages present a remarkable parallel between the Underground Man's narrative and Kierkegaard's analysis. Note, to start with, how the Underground Man's stratagem of "escape" advances from reading through sensuality to self-worship. Man despairs last of wanting to be God—the Underground Man's theology is indeed excellent. His whole style of writing suddenly takes a religious turn. Thus he speaks of a blind belief in some miracle that would save him in an instant, of issuing forth into God's world mounted on a white horse, and as a perfect being extending pardon to wretched sinners groveling before him in the dust. Not even Nietzsche's *Übermensch* could have put things more clearly.

What Kierkegaard calls "experimenting" is for the Underground Man a "way of escape contained in [his] visionary cult of the 'great and the beautiful.'" Kierkegaard's insistence that these experiments are lacking in seriousness is corroborated in the Underground Man's case not only by their failure to bring about a permanent reconciliation but also by the attitude that informs his participation in them. In spite of his sustained reflection over himself in relation to his despair, he continues to believe that "some external circumstance would suddenly

• *The Sickness unto Death,* pp. 200-3.

cause the present to break." And what a utopia he has mapped out for himself! "Mounted on a white horse and crowned with laurels": it is hard to see how this would leave any room for a higher power to view the magnificent spectacle. In Kierkegaard's terms the Underground Man "bestow[s] upon [his] undertakings infinite interest and importance" going so far that "[he] becomes an 'experimental god'" though, it must be added, "[he] remains from first to last the self . . . neither more nor less than the self." Corresponding to "having the fabric finished [the self] can arbitrarily resolve the whole thing into nothing" is the Underground Man's admission that, having "spent more than three months upon these ecstasies of mine . . . I began to feel a renewed inclination for intercourse with my fellow-men." The honeymoon was over.

Not unlike Napoleon in this respect, the Underground Man cherishes these visions of grandeur in which he sees himself rising "superior to all mankind." Without being aware of it, it is here that he puts his finger on the root of his sickness unto death: insatiable pride! Quite properly Kierkegaard relates the entire phenomenon of despair to the doctrine of sin. What does the Underground Man really want to experience? "All men were in the dust before me, and forced to recognize my perfection as I extended to them my pardon." He wants to be god, but a very particular kind of god: his will should be done at everybody else's expense. No mercy, forgiveness, justice, grace, or love is to be expected from his throne. His experiment comes to an end, but the twentieth century has experienced similar instances of real men rising from the underground for considerably longer intervals to explore the possibilities of inhumanity. The death of God, which Nietzsche celebrated as the dawn of a new freedom, turned into the nightmare Dostoevsky and Kierkegaard were already envisaging.

Sin Is Not a Negation but a Position

I have not only invariably failed to recognize as unseemly, but never failed to commit, actions which—well, actions which all men commit, but which I have always perpetrated just when I was most acutely sensible that I ought not to do them. The more I have recognized what is good and what constitutes "the great and the beautiful," the deeper I have plunged into the mire, and the more I have been ready to smear myself over with the sticky stuff. . . . Who was it first said, first propounded the theory, that man does evil only because he is blind to his own interests, but that if he were enlightened, if his eyes were opened to his real, his normal interests, he would at once cease to do evil, and become virtuous and noble for the reason that, being now enlightened and brought to understand what is best for him, he would discern his true advantage only in what is good (since it is a known thing that no man of set purpose acts against his own interests), and therefore would of necessity also *do* what is good? Oh, the simplicity of the youth who said this! Oh, the utter artlessness of the prattler! •

What determinant is it then that Socrates lacks in determining what sin is? It is will, defiant will. The Greek intellectualism was too happy, too naive, too aesthetic, too ironical, too witty . . . too sinful to be able to get it into its head that a person knowingly could fail to do the good, or knowingly, with knowledge of what is right, do what was wrong. The Greek spirit proposes an intellectual categorical imperative. ••

Unlike the Underground Man, Kierkegaard was far from regarding Socrates as a simple youth or artless prattler. In unmistakable disdain of Hegel he looked upon him as the philosopher's philosopher because he never held a chair in philosophy but philosophized in his gadfly fashion in the streets of Athens. The "solitary individual," Kierkegaard, ostracized by complacent contemporaries, often identified his task with the sublime martyrdom of the Greek ironist. This makes his agreement with the Underground Man that sin is a position rather than a negation

• *Letters from the Underworld*, pp. 9-10, 25.
•• *The Sickness unto Death*, pp. 220-1.

profoundly important. In direct opposition to Socrates, Kierkegaard is saying: because their wills are defiant, men are perfectly capable of committing an act that they know to be morally wrong even while carrying it out. Both Dostoevsky and Kierkegaard were Christian voluntarists and thus opposed to the intellectualist assumption dominating the great tradition from Socrates to Kant that the ability of an individual to act in accord with his will hinges on the proper understanding of his own nature and condition. Concerning Kant's categorical imperative, Kierkegaard remarks somewhere that if on each occasion while saying "I ought" man would receive a kick in the pants, the "I can" would surely follow.

The life of the Underground Man obviously refutes any high correlation, let alone necessary connection, between reasoning intelligence and self-redemption through moral action, but apart from this fictional character who might be dismissed as a monstrosity, there have always been great difficulties with the Socratic view of evil as ignorance. No doubt—and Kierkegaard fully acknowledges this—a great deal of moral evil is the result of ignorance. In quest of reasons for disliking someone it is always a fertile field of speculation whether stupidity or meanness should be the ground for one's aversion. A German saying has it that against stupidity even the gods fight in vain. On the other hand, it is equally apparent that intelligence aided by considerable self-understanding is not incompatible with a conscious choice of evil.[24] The Underground Man defines man as an "ungrateful creature." He is also a spiteful one who on occasion would rather act against his previously discerned self-interest if by so doing he can deflate someone else. Not only is Socrates unable to account for this common type of behavior (Kierkegaard would argue because he had no revelation of the Christian notion of sin before God), but he also neglects to consider how ignorance in a human being may be willful rather than natural. He must have realized in the course of his teaching that some individuals he conversed with never opened themselves up to what he had to say, never allowed themselves to be changed by his dialectical "midwifery." And what about those who never came to listen to him, who, speaking figuratively, constitute the majority of the human race? Ignorance of the good in many instances would not seem to be a better excuse than ignorance of the law. Kierkegaard points to Socratic irony with its double meaning of "understanding" as evidence that Socrates was aware of limitations to his view. Men understand matters without understanding them, that is to say, translating them into existential realities, and as a result find themselves in absurd postures. But beyond suggesting this, Socrates could not go. Sin as a determinant of the will was unknown to him and Greek culture generally.[25] (For a famous discussion in Greek philosophy of Socrates' doctrine that virtue is knowledge, see Aristotle's *Nichomachean Ethics,* Book VII, Chapters 2 and 3. While Aristotle makes the same distinction that Kierkegaard makes between "potential" and "actual" knowledge, he concludes "that Socrates' contention is really substantiated.")

The Sin of Despairing over One's Sin

I often told myself that I would greatly like to know whether the same delight fell to the lot of other men. First of all, however, let me explain to you wherein that delight lay. It lay in a clear consciousness of my degradation—in a feeling that I had reached the last wall, and that the whole thing was base, and could never be otherwise, and that no escape therefrom was to be looked for, and that it was not possible for me to become a different man, and that, even if I still retained sufficient faith and energy to become a different man, I should not wish to become so, but that I would rather do nothing at all in the matter, since to undergo such a change might not be worthwhile. . . . Hence may be deduced the fact that oversensibility causes a villain to hug his villainy to himself if he really perceives that he is a villain. •

Despair over sin is an attempt to maintain oneself by sinking still deeper. As one who ascends in a

• *Letters from the Underworld,* pp. 10-11.

balloon rises by casting weights from him, so does the despairing man sink by casting from him the good (for the weight of the good is uplift), he sinks—doubtless, he thinks he is rising—he does indeed become lighter. Sin itself is the struggle of despair; but when strength is exhausted there must needs be a new potentiation, a new demoniacal introversion, and this is despair over one's sin. . . . This despair does not will to be itself with Stoic doting upon itself, nor with self-deification, willing in this way, doubtless mendaciously, yet in a certain sense in terms of its perfection; no, with hatred for existence it wills to be itself, to be itself in terms of its misery; it does not even in defiance or defiantly will to be itself, but to be itself in spite; it does not even will in defiance to tear itself free from the Power which posited it, it wills to obtrude upon this power in spite, to hold on to it out of malice. •

Note once again how the development of the Underground Man's despair is illuminated by Kierkegaard's phenomenology: having despaired over the world and himself and sought escape successively in "higher pleasures," "lower pleasures," illusions of grandeur— experiments at being god—he now reaches the conclusion that since he cannot become a different man he does not even wish to do so, preferring to do nothing at all except "hug his villainy to himself." Thus he himself explains his contemptible treatment of Liza. Kierkegaard defines this kind of despair as "a new demoniacal introversion. . . . With hatred for existence it wills to be itself, to be itself in terms of its misery." No longer holding out hope for any change in his condition, the Underground Man as despairer has nothing to lose by doing what he pleases, however monstrous and diabolical the heights of his folly. To be without illusions is rightly reckoned as a desirable state for human beings, but to be without hope—a state actually attained by a few thinkers since the early nineteenth century—is, quite aside from the accompanying intensity of despair, an invitation to grotesque destructiveness. An intellectualist theory of ethics would argue that

• *The Sickness unto Death*, pp. 207, 241.

being free from illusions is far more difficult than being devoid of hope, inasmuch as the former demands rare perceptiveness while the latter requires no particular talent whatsoever. Anybody, on this view, can give up hope if the pinch of existence gets too tight. From the Christian point of view, the state of disillusionment is comparatively easy to enter into, given a minimum capacity for reflection. But hopefulness or hopelessness— there is the rub. For the Underground Man to despair over his sin is, in the Christian sense, a tremendous accomplishment: few men among those free from illusions have the courage to sink still deeper "by casting from [them] the good." Such action, horrible as it is, makes far greater claims on the individual than building castles in the air or touching things up with ephemeral sweetness and light. It is always the dialectical advantage of the nihilist over the philistine to be spirited and a little bit more honest with himself. There is a genuine sense, as it were, in which Hitler's supporters were guiltier than their idol. The Underground Man, this much must be said for him, would not have stood on his ignorance or his right of security. He despaired "bravely."

Giving himself up to malice now becomes his sole refuge. In a harangue full of self-pity and self-torment he accuses Liza[26] of having come to his apartment with ulterior motives, and proceeds to add fuel to the fire by asserting that he had been "playing" with her all along. Thereupon he reveals himself to her as a foul unseemly creature without any discernible relation to the hero figure he supposes she must have imagined him to be after their encounter in the brothel. How could he possibly save Liza, he remarks with a logic no less coherent than that informing his previous sermon on the virtues of matrimony, if his need for salvation is so much greater than hers? But having confided this he will hate her for the rest of his life:

> Nor shall I ever be able to pardon you the reason why I am confessing this to you. . . . Other worms may be no better than I am, yet at least, for some God-only-known reason, they seem never to look

foolish as I do, who all my life shall have to be
slapped on the cheek by lice, since that is my *metier*.
But what does it matter to you whether you understand this or not? And what does it matter to me
whether you meet your ruin in this house or not? And
cannot you understand, that, having told you all this,
I shall for ever hate you for having heard it? Man but
once in his life makes such confessions as mine, and
then only when he is in a fit of hysteria. And, after it
all, how is it that you are still to flout and torture me,
instead of taking your departure? [27]

Kierkegaard views the relationship of despairer (the
Underground Man) to confidant (Liza) as follows:

Poetically the catastrophe (assuming . . . that the
protagonist was e.g. a king or emperor) might be
fashioned in such a way that the hero had the confidant put to death. One could imagine such a
demoniacal tyrant who felt the need of talking to a
fellow man about his torment, and this way consumed
successively a whole lot of men; for to be his
confidant was certain death.—It would then be the
task of a poet to represent this agonizing self-contra-
diction in a demoniac man who is not able to get
along without a confidant, and not able to have a
confidant, and then resolving it in such a way as
this. [28]

The Underground Man cannot consume himself because
of his sickness unto death. In order to relieve his over-
wrought mind and vindicate his corrupted heart he
requires a confidant who must be spiritually healthier
than himself to listen to him lovingly and patiently but—
and here is a contradiction—who must be literally self-
effacing, who must not remind him of her spiritual superiority in this regard. [29] Liza certainly is not a woman
unacquainted with suffering and vice. She would be the
last to judge the Underground Man from Olympian heights
of middle-class respectability. She knows also what it means
to be in despair, and has told him so about herself. Ironically enough, it is her being her kindhearted and open self
that drives him to paroxysms of hatred. He cannot tolerate
direct confrontation by a person who—without abstracting

herself into the role of magnificent sinner—has had to put up with at least as much concrete misery as he himself. So, harboring his touchiness as the last defense against authentic exposure (conversion), he is offended by Liza's selflessness and placidity, especially following his confession. Offense, according to Kierkegaard, is a mixture of admiration and envy. "An admirer who feels that he cannot be happy by surrendering himself elects to become envious of that which he admires. So he speaks another language, and in that language of his the thing which he really admires is called stupid, insipid, and a queer sort of thing." [30] He is really a great admirer of Liza, but his habitual attitude toward all of existence being hatred and offense—he is forever offended and insulted by the smallest trifle—and his demoniac despair having passed the point of no return, he discards her from the ken of his existence. His sin of despairing over sin takes the form of rejecting the only person who he knows loves him as he cannot love himself.

The Sin of Despairing of the Forgiveness of Sins

To me, love connotes tyrannisation and moral ascendancy. Any other love has never come within my purview, and I have even gone so far as to arrive at the firm conclusion that, properly speaking, love lies in the peculiar right of tyrannisation which the fact of being loved confers. Even in my most secret soul I have never been able to think of love as aught but a struggle which begins with hatred and ends with moral subjection. •

When a sinner despairs of the forgiveness of sins it is almost as if he were directly picking a quarrel with God, it sounds in effect like a rejoinder when he says, "No, there is not any forgiveness of sins, it is an impossibility. . . ." On the whole it is unbelieveable what confusion has invaded the religious sphere since in man's relationship to God there has been abolished the "Thou shalt," which is the only regulative principle. This "Thou shalt" ought to be a part of every definition of the religious; instead of which

• *Letters from the Underworld*, p. 144.

people have employed fantastic conceptions of God
as an ingredient in human self-importance, so as to
be self-important over against God. •

The greatest and hardest (it has been called the "impossible imperative") Christian commandment is "Thou shalt
love"—God, neighbor, and even enemy. It is fitting that
the Underground Man can only visualize love as tyran-
nization, the exact opposite of agape. What Kierkegaard
equates with despair of the forgiveness of sins, namely,
"picking a quarrel with God," corresponds to the Underground Man's confession: "never at any time have I
found it possible to say, 'Father forgive me, and I will
sin no more.' I always found it irksome to sit with folded
hands." [31] Thus he places himself beyond the pale of even
that redemptive Power for whom the impossible can
become possible. Is there any better refutation of
Nietzsche's identification of strength with self-assertion
and of weakness with compassion?

Dostoevsky's portrait of the Underground Man ranks
with Shakespeare's Macbeth, Milton's Satan, and Melville's Captain Ahab as one of the supreme characteri-
zations of despair in Western literature. The Underground
Man also experienced life "as a tale told by an idiot
signifying nothing," but the manner in which he arrived
at his apprehension was quite different from Macbeth's.
Where Shakespeare's hero succumbed to the hubris of the
Renaissance, unbridled ambition, the Underground Man's
defiance was rooted in boredom and anxiety. Feeling
deserted by God and having withdrawn from Him on his
own volition, his experiments with being "god" are intended to cover up the pervasive threat of meaninglessness
not only in his life, but in modern life generally. That is
the main reason for the effectiveness of Dostoevsky's conception of his situation: while timeless it lights up our
times with perspicacity and depth matched alone perhaps
by Kierkegaard's authorship. Just as Dostoevsky's Underground Man turned out to be a forerunner of the tortured

• *The Sickness unto Death*, pp. 245-6.

souls in Kafka and Camus, so is Kierkegaard's dialectical theology the prototypal embodiment of virtually every major current in twentieth-century religious thought. What then, it would naturally occur to many, brings the Underground Man's mode of existence and the categories of Kierkegaard's theological thinking into such close agreement? The Underground Man's mode of existence testifies to the death of God and its consequences, which Western society has alternately bemoaned and plotted since the Enlightenment, and Kierkegaard's theology constitutes the seminal work of reflection, by a religious man, on this plotted or bemoaned eclipse of God and its ominous significance for Western civilization. So it comes about that *The Sickness unto Death* is the finest commentary on *Letters from the Underworld*.

CHAPTER V

The Breakdown of Faith:
Seven Types of Offense

For instance, I have often been *careful* to take offense at something—not for any good reason, but merely because I wanted to. Gentlemen, you yourselves know that if one takes causeless offense—the sort of offense which one brings upon oneself—one ends by being really, and in every truth, offended.
Fyodor Dostoevsky[1]

Next to despair the most characteristic mood of the Underground Man is the feeling of offense—his aggregate of resentments reinforcing and in turn feeding upon his unhappiness. All men are ever offended by virtue of envisaging possibilities incompatible with reality, but since the latter half of the eighteenth century Western man in particular seems to have become extraordinarily sensitive to the slights of nature and history, and predisposed to invoke the absurdity of existence on every conceivable ground. When Marx uttered his prophetic words to the effect of changing the world instead of being content to contemplate it, he consciously broke with a long tradition of Stoic acceptance and Christian forbearance. The "chain of being" was broken. Ever since, a procession of "outsiders" and underground men has ventured forth to make earth a paradise. Still, doubt prevails whether the resentment of Nietzsche's supermen and Marx's proletariat will yield any more readily to changes in the environment than the Underground Man's spite. As Dostoevsky observed with his usual keenness, man has an infinite capacity for

being offended even when he cannot put his finger on a
specific grievance.

The best-known type of offense in the modern world is
not that of the Cross, but of capitalism. This in turn can
be subsumed under injustice, which may further be
classified as a species of unconnected matter of fact.[2]
Whether justice is a tentative possibility or merely a
dream, historical man has been consistently aware of
dwelling in an unjust universe. From the Book of Job
to Hume's *Dialogues Concerning Natural Religion*[3] the
indifference and downright hostility of nature to human
aspirations has been exhaustively analyzed, bemoaned,
and catalogued. Where Hume broke with tradition was in
discarding the inscrutable workings of a higher Power as
an explanatory hypothesis. (Unlike Job, Philo could not
make such an act of faith.) Nor, in his treatment of social
evil, was Marx as revolutionary as has sometimes been
supposed. Long before the coming of industrialism,
Plato's *Republic* provided a superb account of mutual
human exploitation. There probably was no time when
one group in a particular community did not for some
good reason feel alienated from the others. What distinguishes Marxism (aside from its analysis of slavery and
freedom in terms of poverty and wealth) is not particularly
its recognition of resentment on the part of the "outs"
against the "ins," but its anti-stoical call to action: the
proletariat are invited to throw off their chains even
if this requires recourse to violence. Class warfare can
be brought to an end only by its perpetuation. Eventually,
with the proletariat victorious, Marx anticipated a society
free from mutual exploitation. If only he had desisted from
confusing apocalyptic expectations with scientific pre-
dictions he might have spared subsequent generations
much disillusionment. Had he read his contemporary,
Kierkegaard, he would have learned that false pride and
humiliation, far from being confined to a single powerful
class at any one time, are as universal as sin and despair.
The poor no less than the rich crave to regard themselves
as masters of their fate, and when reality threatens this
illusion, both nurse their grievances and look for another

party to whom to transmit the insult. Hurt pride is par
and parcel of the human condition, although it is true tha
sometimes money can be instrumental in mitigating it
pain.

Like so many categories of our time, "offense" came int
general usage by way of theology, more specifically
through the writings of Kierkegaard. In *Training in Chris
tianity* and *Attack Upon Christendom* he contrasts th
folly of the Cross with the diluted faith of Christendom
This folly or offense rests essentially on the incongruity o
the way of Jesus (to the Cross) with the way of th
world—the instincts and desires of natural man. Kierke
gaard's more timely point seems to be that the kind o
self-fulfillment humanists had advocated since the Renais
sance, either as complementary to the Christian faith o
presumably coinciding with it, cannot do justice to th
suffering and self-denial explicit in the New Testamen
narrative. Above all, Kierkegaard insisted on honesty
What inspired his polemic was not so much the perennia
fact of nominal Christianity in the world as the particu
larly obnoxious hypocrisy of the bourgeoisie. The
rising middle class had an irrepressible need for falsifica
tion: on the material plane this manifested itself in the
familiar exhibitionism of the *nouveaux riches,* on the
spiritual in the convenient compromises of Christendom.
Thus Christianity turned out to be the ideal religion for
sanctioning the accumulation of property. Kierkegaard,
with bitter irony and Socratic exaggeration, set out to
show how unnatural and unreasonable and unyielding
Jesus really was over against middle-class standards of
propriety. Apart from this, it is no mystery that man is
as easily offended by kindliness and love as by asperity,
especially when his desires remain unsatisfied.

The offense of *unsatisfied desire* is the most basic and
recurring type in human experience. The child who does
not get his will and bursts into tears, the man unrequited
in love, the woman unprovided with all the things she
thinks she ought to have—these are characteristic
instances of it. Whether we show or hide the fact, all of us

profess cravings that cannot be satisfied. The reason for this state of affairs may be that circumstance is against us or that society represses our private wishes for a good we may not at first, if ever, be able to see and share. Though the head can come to recognize the unattainability of appetites and desires, our whole being tends to be offended regardless. "Perhaps the stupid occasion of our change of quarters pursued us to the new ones we had found," writes the narrator of "Mario and the Magician." "Personally, I admit that I do not easily forget these collisions with ordinary humanity, the naïve misuse of power, the injustice, the sycophantic corruption. I dwelt upon the incident too much, it irritated me in retrospect —quite futilely, of course, since such phenomena are only all too natural and all too much the rule." [4] At the moment of frustration we are persuaded that we ought not to be frustrated, whatever the nature of our demands upon reality. With respect to the offense of unsatisfied desire it matters little whether or not the desire can be judged legitimate. An old man brooding over his lost youth is as offended by the passing of time as an exploited member of society waiting to get to the top. There is no correlation between degree of offense and degree of injustice. Wounded pride makes no such distinctions.

Since the satisfaction of one desire often results in the eruption of another, philosophers have spoken of the paradox of unsatisfied desire, meaning that to be human is to be perpetually dissatisfied—either saturated or athirst. Both the letdown that follows realization and the anxiety that attends it bear witness to the frustrated condition of mankind. Is there a "specious present" in which man is free from the dread of anticipation as well as from the depression of success, or are we driven back and forth between these uneasy moods? Happiness is where one is not, remarked Goethe with characteristic sagacity; and that other seminal mind for the nineteenth century, Kant, postponed the marriage of virtue and happiness until an indefinite future beyond this life. Though the offense of unsatisfied desire has its roots in the universal experience of frustration, its acuteness in modern thought emerges as a special datum. Since the middle of the eighteenth century, notwithstanding the marvels of science and social reform, there has been heard a swelling chorus of weariness and trepidation. It would be pleasant to agree with Sir Harold Nicolson[5] that this was merely a symptom of protracted adolescence induced by Romanticism.

A more reflective type of offense is that of *unconnected matters of fact*. Man need not reflect to have inordinate or frustrated desires, but understanding the world as meaningless, unjust, indifferent, or malevolent presupposes some deliberation on experience beyond, in Dostoevsky's phrase, "the capacity for receiving impressions." Metaphysics and religion have served for thousands of years—alas, in vain—to remove this particular "offense" from our apprehension of reality. The mind of man cannot tolerate an external world seemingly devoid of all purpose, if not inimical to human realization of any sort. Nature's neutrality is an affront, especially to our moral faculties. Some men have resigned themselves to the unaccountable facets of experience, though rarely without a note of bitterness or disenchantment entering into their lives as a result. Others have assumed that it is entirely up to us what we make of life. Thus meaninglessness is attributed to our failure to make things meaningful by developing the appropriate attitudes toward them: if you don't expect anything, you won't be disappointed. No doubt, individuals have been enabled to sustain the hardest blows in this manner, yet it remains difficult to see how the daemonic aspects of human contingency and history, for example, are resolved by calling them something else or pretending they do not exist. For unless we are prepared to suspend our notions of righteousness and goodness in the face of brute fact, the incommensurability of what objectively transpires with alternative and more sensible possibilities remains an irreducible datum. From an abstract point of view, everything may be seen to conspire together to produce the greatest quantity of good; but such a vision, even where seriously entertained, fails to bridge the chasm between life and thought in concrete situations.

Unable to support rationalists, empiricists, and naturalists in their endeavor to make the offense of unconnected matters of fact a pseudoproblem in philosophy, many of the existentialist thinkers decided on it as the cornerstone of their philosophizing. Thrown into a world they experienced fundamentally as blind and deceitful, the traditional arguments and consolations being no longer efficacious, they desperately strove to evolve a new philosophy. As the offense of unsatisfied desire in modern literature is symptomatic of a pervasive Romanticism that may be said to have reached a climax with Rousseau, the offense of unconnected matters of fact is, in its radical manifestations since the Enlightenment, an outgrowth of an uninterrupted spiritual crisis. Dostoevsky's novels are filled with characters who, with little expectation of finding any answer, probe relentlessly, even masochistically, the mysteries of human existence. The hero of *Letters from the Underworld* is— taking due account of his personal pathology—the conscience of modern thought. Either he tries to ignore what he hates to be bothered with or he indulges in the wildest speculations and actions, meanwhile despising himself on both counts. But apart from the extremes toward which the offense of unconnected matters of fact has gravitated in Marx's allegedly scientific philosophy of history, in the aberrations of much modern art and music, in the devil-worship of the French symbolists and the appeal of theosophy, it has always been present in human life. So long as man thinks, he must rebel against his fate of finding himself in an incomprehensible order. Because he had faith Job did not develop a philosophy of the absurd, though he was quite familiar with the kind of experience that gave rise to it in Camus. Only recognition of unconnected matters of fact for what they are (Hume), and their acceptance for human existence (Freud and psychotherapy), can theoretically eliminate this offense. But it is extremely doubtful that human beings will ever act accordingly, or even that they should. If man is self-transcending, such acceptance, while mitigating suffering of one variety, will accentuate another through guilt. For how can a creature not solely of this world absolutize it without self-betrayal? The tragic drama is unthinkable without this offense. *Oedipus* and *King Lear* have as their common theme the mystery of abused innocence.

The offense of *particularism and exclusivism* is familiar to everyone who, justly or arbitrarily, has been excluded from a group: to the schoolboy ostracized by the regular gang on account of his frailty, to the proletarian worker snubbed by his white-collar foreman, to the nonconformist consigned beyond the pale of salvation, to the member of a so-called "inferior" race discriminated against by his "superiors." In nineteenth-century thought Marxism, racism, nationalism, imperialism, as well as Romantic ideologies made much of the differences that set groups and individuals apart, even encouraging elites that—it came to be argued—were predestined to lord it over those unfit to determine their own destiny. While this type of thinking was patently opposed to the democratic ideal, its hold on all classes of Western society should not be underestimated. Bizarre class-consciousness was not confined to the British, the socialists, and the ultraroyalists, nor can its pervasiveness be accounted for merely on political and economic grounds. The novels of Mann, Thackeray, Proust, and the great Russian writers clearly indicate the unreasoning pride that often motivated the offensive behavior both of the aristocracy and of the middle classes. Whether it was the idealization of making and preserving fortunes, of talent necessarily distributed to but a few, of a genteel way of life or hereditary line, it invariably exceeded most bounds of decency and compassion for those who did not belong. Marx with his vindictive hatred for the bourgeoisie hardly stood on stronger moral footing than the enemy he worked to depose. Tolerance in the modern world was never the simple phenomenon so many liberals took it to be. In practice bigotry and democracy have often made mutual peace. The most ardent lover of the people is prone to reveal himself as contemptuous of individual rights.

Curiously enough, the same class that developed a just reputation for snobbery and intense nationalism was prepared to extend the blessings of Christianity to anyone with a sound moral sense. It was largely against this attitude toward salvation that Kierkegaard launched his attack on Christendom. Why was it, one wonders, that the very people who stimulated particularism and exclusivism in literature, politics, and society were unwilling to face up to the straight and narrow path spelled out for them in the New Testament? An answer that suggests itself at once is that people regard as "exclusive" only those aspects of their lives which concern them ultimately. Today there are still many Christians who, on the one hand, cannot abide the notion of a closed salvation (predestination), but on the other will not even listen to anyone who does not fully share their political and cultural presuppositions. This inconsistency between the acceptance of particularism for certain spheres of activity and its repudiation for others is an illuminating clue to our present spiritual condition. The ideal of making everything worth-while accessible to everybody is fine so long as it is kept in mind that not everybody desires everything worth-while and that many will corrupt and vulgarize what they cannot understand. When Shakespeare wrote his Sonnets and Bach his *Art of the Fugue*, neither, surely, was discriminating against the masses, but such works are meaningful to but a few in any age.

The offense of particularism and exclusivism is, like the other types already delineated, a universally present feature of human existence, resting on the obvious proposition that all men are unequal in many respects and that their lives by choice or dire necessity reflect this inequality at every turning. Far more exacerbating than natural inequality are the varieties imposed on individuals by society. In either case resentment, jealousy, rebelliousness, and hatred are recurring moods aroused in those outside of something which they feel they ought to be in. Whether or not this common reaction is warranted by the facts must be decided on the merits of each case in accordance with principles that are rarely self-evident. If this were under discussion here, one would have to show, for instance, in what sense an organization is entitled to act prejudicially in selecting its members. Immediately relevant are particularism and exclusivism as elements in the Christian scheme of redemption and in religion generally. In emphasizing "offense" as a necessary condition for understanding the meaning of the Cross, Kierkegaard touches on a central motif in the New Testament, and one not absent from the Old. Following Christ as depicted in the Gospels is hardly commensurate with yielding to a natural instinct. Nor are the facts related in the Gospels free from paradox and questionable moral sensitivity. Jesus was not a popular hero. If he suggested in some of his sayings that all of mankind might be saved, in others he made it plain that only those could enter the "kingdom" who chose to accept his terms for doing so, making it quite clear that he did not expect the majority to take that option. He offended against family feeling in the treatment of his mother, against natural knowledge in his performance of miracles, against meekness in his anger at the barren fig tree, against justice in not explaining himself before Pilate. Add to this the Christology of the Gospels—Christ is at once exalted and humiliated—and there cannot be much doubt that most of us would feel like Ivan or the Grand Inquisitor if our experience of Christianity were anything but vicarious.

In building up his case against Christendom, Kierkegaard virtually ignored those features of New Testament Christianity which, it might be said, deepen the offense even further than his indictment is apt to disclose. Thus Jesus not only denied the world but also came to give life here and now; not only did he accept suffering but also ministered to sufferers; not only did he single out the poor, hurt, and insulted for his attentions but also defended the relative luxury of having his body well cared for—contrary to the evangelical communism of some of his critics. In brief, Jesus is invariably more complex and less intelligible than even his profoundest interpreters make him out to be. Kierkegaard was right in his insistence that those who are not offended by him at all cannot bear witness to his truth, but the offense he concentrated on in his analysis circumscribed but one of many discernible layers. A corrective should not be expected to take the place of a balanced view, and Kierkegaard brilliantly surmised that a balanced view of everything, including the Christian faith, had become the chief idol of his generation, behind whose respectability many hid from confrontation and commitment. Considering the fact that he addressed himself to a Christendom in which everyone felt Christian by virtue of consumption and belonging, his attack was most appropriate.

Particularism and exclusivism are so easily abhorred these days that they require a defense. Archetypal here is the inconsistency of liberals who cry out against any "chosen people" and then talk only to one another. More important, nothing great is everybody's cup of tea. Be it the Buddhist, Christian, or Socratic way of life, it is folly to suppose that it exercises a universal claim. When such a claim is put forward it must properly be judged as potential rather than actual. The possibility of becoming a Christian is an act of grace freely bestowed, never a necessity. Religions do compete with each other for our allegiance, and the ensuing tensions set up in our minds by this embarrassing situation must be struggled with as other tensions must be. If everyone naturally sought salvation, all religions would be superfluous. And the same, incidentally, applies to the domains of education and art. Mainly because an individual is offended by his own ignorance does he set out in quest of authentic knowledge. And many men obviously are not thus offended. Not everyone loves Bach and Shakespeare, but why should the nonlovers be envious of those who do and the lovers condescending toward those who do not? The worldly tragedy of Christianity and other "narrow ways" has been to translate genuine particularism into persecution. But there is no inevitable connection between them. Kierkegaard, for example, never voiced a theological hatred of non-Christians. He could not abide Christians who pretended to be what they were not. What they actually were was their own business before God. Men will always will different ends, and it is sad but not improbable that what most of them desire will bring neither happiness nor peace. The illusions and lies that alienate nations and individuals do not cancel the real differences between them. Each of us is genuinely offended by his loneliness in a dangerous world.

A fourth type of offense is confrontation by *saintliness*. Analogous to the anticipations of boredom aroused in our moral natures by the Christian heaven is the pique and cynicism with which we are prone to regard purity of heart in a fellow human being. The complete absence of ulterior motives is even more difficult to fathom than the ways of the devil. Dostoevsky's classical depictions of innocence in Prince Myshkin, Sonia, Liza, and Father Zossima emphasize the uneasiness they stirred up in all those with whom they came into contact. Individuals who defy measurement by our standards make us feel angry notwithstanding the possibility that we secretly revere them. This is especially true of saints whose external appearance and occasional eccentricity of behavior seem to belie their status. The note of ill-suppressed glee in our frequent admission that to be human is to err, that everyone has his faults, that without our weaknesses we would be uninteresting, is inescapable. Not only is the uncompromising idealist impractical and clumsy in going about his affairs, but much of the time he seems to misunderstand matters. The Grand Inquisitor knew whereof he spoke in observing that the ecclesiastical establishment had done an infinitely superior job in organizing the means of salvation. No wonder he found the reappearance of Jesus on earth such a nuisance. And so would we. Saintly conduct is basically unintelligible. It always implies a "transvaluation of values" which collides with common sense and habits. Hence Kant dissociated a holy will from moral beings. God alone is purely good, beyond good and evil. But in Christianity the Word became flesh, and mortal saints became a possibility. Perfectionism wounds us where we are most vulnerable, in our assumption that a life regarded as respectable by the best minds and standards of the day should not be subject to sudden revision. Aristotle's golden mean is difficult enough to live up to as it is. Goodness exceeding that is "offense," save in a wish or in a dream.

Though an extreme form of unsatisfied desire, the offense of *death* deserves special mention because, more unmistakably than any other stage on life's way, it exposes human contingency. Men are often judged by how they died, and our attitude towards death is a reliable index to what we really believe life is for. For the individual on the point of death it is virtually impossible to simulate a metaphysic. Tolstoy in *The Death of Ivan Ilyitch* has given us the deepest view of death in all modern literature: Ivan's unwillingness to face it, his terror when it can no longer be gotten out of his mind, his desperate clinging to familiar surroundings (however oppressive they were under ordinary circumstances), the merciless finality of his end—these are universal reactions to the phenomenon. What is so offensive about death, apart from the pain and suffering that often accompany its coming, is the implicit threat of meaninglessness. Why make so much fuss about living if all must come to this? Death does in fact tend to make us look ridiculous with our petty worries and commotions, our preoccupation with trifles as if our lives depended on them. Even where death is experienced as the gateway to possible eternal life, it does not lose its sting as an inescapable limiting concept for our mortal selves. Socrates is reported to have died cheerfully, but his friends were distraught, and Plato caught their mood in his marvelous account.

How powerfully death brings home to us the proneness to accident attending our most carefully laid plans, the brutal interruption of the highest love pledged unto eternity, the instability of our firmest foundations. Stoicism and certain varieties of modern naturalism do not recognize death as offensive. Everything that lives dies as naturally as it came into being. But man is not merely natural. He knows that he must die, as Pascal put it, and hence death for him is qualitatively different from death for a flower or a dog. Moreover, the cultivation of equanimity, imperturbability, and aloofness does not alter the objective character of death as the irreversible separation from life as we know it, whatever comfort these virtues may give us in accepting it courageously. Since the Enlightenment the traditional priority attached to permanence as a necessary condition for genuine experience has often been questioned. Why not enjoy each fleeting moment, including the moment of death? Eternity is undramatic in any event. But human beings who do not wish to be separated from those who love them and whom they love, who Hamlet-like are more anxious about the unexplored than the experienced mysteries, find small comfort in such consolations. For death strikes us at least a little bit uncommonsensical. Although Christianity is the religion of the Resurrection, death, the human death of God, is the pivotal event in the Gospels. And Jesus himself dying on the Cross was offended by death: "My God, my God, why hast thou forsaken me?"

Some critics of Romanticism and its next of kin, existentialism, maintain that the crisis-thinking of the twentieth century is but another in a series of literary celebrations of adolescence going back to the end of the Enlightenment. In other words, so their argument runs, being unable to take things at their face value, you wax emotional over them and become prey to a vicious circle of false hopes, fears, regrets, and faiths. If only Blake, Dostoevsky, Kierkegaard, Marx, Nietzsche and their disciples would suppress some of their infinite passion and gaze on reality with the sanguine coolness of a Hume, they and we would have been spared a great deal of superfluous pain. This line of criticism is not to be confused with the conventional strictures on sentimentality and overwroughtness, nor does it fall under the kind of doctrinaire naturalism that views man as the most intricate machine on earth. The offense of *infinite passion*, the dialectical contrary of the offense of *unconnected matters of fact*, is quite compatible with the recognition of man as a self-transcending creature, so long as this element of self-transcendence is kept in check, not allowed to intrude more than indistinguishably into our apprehension of things. Whereas those offended by unconnected matters of fact will show the greatest respect for what they feel reality ought to be rather than what it is, those offended by infinite passion will invoke Stoic acceptance as their guide. In all the confusion of modern schools of thought the breakdown of Stoicism and its stepbrother, Christianity, is perhaps their most conspicuous common feature. Existentialist, Marxist, scientific atheist—all these are bent on revolutionizing existence. Their impatience clashes sharply with the equanimity of the sage who subordinates his passional and volitional nature to the initial rhythm of the universe. In this sense, Marx was no less a Romantic than Byron.

The offense of infinite passion, though a desirable corrective to certain excesses of Romanticism, has in turn given rise to a cult of objectivism which is pernicious in its own way. What Ortega y Gasset called the dehumanization of man is in part this attempt to isolate the idealizing and emotive faculties from apprehension posited here as purely cognitive. The antithesis of the Romantic who thinks with his heart and feels with his head is the person who appreciates with his senses and understands with his brain. Much of the dryness and dreariness in contemporary music and scholarship can be attributed to a fear and revulsion from the creative powers of man. He who is deeply offended by Keats's imagery or a Schumann melody (and there are many today) is inclined to condemn subjectivity as ruinous and deceiving. But why? Because they are insufficiently symbolic or complex? What false sophistication! Is it not partly because he is afraid to come to terms with his own subjectivity, like the middle-aged Goethe turning his back on the best of his lyrical poetry? As viewed from Mars, the twentieth-century scene is probably no more absurd than the high Middle Ages, but for a human being living and thinking in either period, this is hardly the question. The offense of infinite passion, in modern life, is an inverted escapism from the problem of meaning, an escapism whose wide currency and respectability in our day is by way of rationalization curiously linked to the phenomenal success of the natural sciences. Even where man seeks to understand himself as pure object, he remains subject, "listening with the third ear." And insofar as he is subject, he is infinitely passionate because that is his nature. Plato, whom few would accuse of Romanticism in the bad sense, resorted to myth to bridge the gulf between the world as it really seems to be and the world in which man has his being. Biblical revelation is a variant of this fundamental human need for transcendence. To be genuine, the offense of infinite passion requires the offense of unconnected matters of fact as its handmaiden. Together they describe man's ambivalent relationship to his world.

The seventh type of offense is the offense of *faith,* not only of the Christian faith, which in recent years has become familiar enough through Kierkegaard and the Barthians, but of faith in general. Faith in the sense of trust and confidence is already offensive to us because the struggle for existence discourages it and tends to make it look ridiculous. The shrewd and worldly man trusts nothing and nobody save a lucky break. Though this is partly a manner of speaking, any movement of faith is opposed to sheer calculation, while getting along well in this world depends primarily on the systematic pursuit of enlightened self-interest. Of course, the individual who prides himself on not trusting anybody or anything unless his evidence is complete, besides being inconsistent, cuts himself off from a great number of experiences—such as love—that are inconceivable within a strict Machiavellian framework. Hume, James, and Santayana, none of whom can be accused of religious orthodoxy, affirmed in common the indispensability of faith, be it in the existence of the external world, in the possibility of happiness, or in a realm of essences integral to reality. But modern man in particular, as James rightly saw, is reluctant to profess any greater degree of faith than is essential for him to survive. Our recoil in religion from dogma, in science from certainty, and in morals from commitment is part of the same nexus of tentativeness and relativism which after a liberating phase threatens to tyrannize over us in turn. In James's previously cited *aperçu,* we have reached a point where we would rather be damned than make a mistake.[6] This is as evident today in the kind of pedantic scholarship that lays primary stress on correct footnotes (accuracy over subject matter) as in much of contemporary philosophy (the right use of language over having anything to communicate). If one's faith is confined to the primitive concepts of a system, one should not expect to say anything, and certainly one should not deprecate faith, for then even the primitive concepts disappear and one has absolutely nothing.

Blind faith, meaning acquiescence in unexamined propositions as true, has justly been contested with vigor in thought since the seventeenth century. But faith as the admission of dependence on presuppositions and data without which we could not begin to be critical; as willingness to trust another human being though his trustworthiness is beyond the pale of strict determination; faith in the Jamesian sense (where evidence by itself is inadequate to decide) of taking a risk on a forced option; in the Kierkegaardian sense of a heightened level of spirituality attained only by a *leap,* by tearing ourselves away from what is comfortable and accustomed —such faith continues to make claims upon us. Nothing great is in fact accomplished without faith. Without it we could not get married, or plan a long-range project, or devote ourselves to an unpopular cause of whose rightness we are convinced. Faith in these instances means risk-taking, putting oneself out—short of assurances of success or gain—becoming interested in spite of indifference. Its offensiveness lies precisely in the insecurity inseparable from it. Jesus performed miracles only for those who laid themselves open to grave disappointment and mockery by believing in him. It is commonsensical not to believe in miracles or miracle-workers. And yet, one of the parodoxical features of Western man in the twentieth century is his fundamental irreligiousness *combined with* an infinite capacity for living false Absolutes. Ours is both an age of analysis and an age of ideology—witness the recent faith of the American public in Charles Van Doren as an intellectual god.

The offense of faith, then, is rooted in our preference for security and predictability instead of venturesomeness and contingency. We do not relish unprecedented confrontations that may compel us to scrap our whole mode of existence. To be sure, faith in what makes us content with ourselves and enables us to pursue a single course without interference, we spontaneously realize in our activities. As soon as faith means following a will other than our accustomed one, we shrink away from it, often into an all too plausible suspiciousness and worldly caution. Faith in Jesus as the Saviour of mankind presents special problems over which theologians, notably Kierkegaard in modern times, have pondered deeply. The point is that the radical offense that the great Danish thinker stressed in his interpretation of New Testament Christianity may be unique in degree with respect to the infant-God helpless in the cradle and with respect to Christ thirsty on the Cross, but not in kind with respect to others. The foolishness of the Cross is an archetypal foolishness of which many lesser instances can be found in human experience. How many leaps in the dark do we take each day in order to get through it? The mere recognition that appearance is not reality constitutes offense enough.

The seven types of offense are always with us. It is our attitude towards them, both individually and as members of groups, which helps illuminate the ethos of an era. Still in the minds of many today, science will gradually remove the offense of unsatisfied desire; aided and abetted by liberalism and democracy it will transform this world into an inoffensive gadget-paradise. Death, if not conquered, will be indefinitely postponed, class differences will disappear, frustrations will evaporate, faith will be proved beyond doubt (thanks to the philosophy of religion), saints and prophets will be venerated during their lifetime (also geniuses—true ones, that is), and all passion will be directed toward constructive and manageable enterprises. Aldous Huxley has vividly shown us how deodorizers and remarkable improvements in sanitation have in fact exterminated many traditional offenses. But even should the ideal society of the future come into being, there remains Dostoevsky's Underground Man: "Gentlemen, you yourselves know that if one takes causeless offense—the sort of offense which one brings upon oneself—one ends by being really, and in every truth, offended."

CHAPTER VI

The Breakdown of Virtue:
The Teleological Suspension of the Ethical

Clem had a peculiar theory with regard to his own rights and those of the class to which he considered that he belonged. He always held implicitly and sometimes explicitly that gifted people live under a kind of dispensation of grace; the law existing solely for dull souls. What in a clown is a crime punishable by the laws of the land might in a man of genius be a necessary development, or at any rate an excusable offense. He had nothing to say for the servant girl who had sinned with the shopman, but if the artist or poet were to carry off another man's wife, it might not be wrong. He believed, and acted upon the belief, that the inferior ought to render perpetual incense to the superior, and that the superior should receive it as a matter of course.

Mark Rutherford's Deliverance[1]

Another of Kierkegaard's arresting concepts closely related to "offense" is the "teleological suspension of the ethical," the transgression of moral principle in "fear and trembling" as required and justified by religious faith. Communicating indirectly through Johannes de Silentio, who, characteristic of bystanders, is at once incredulous and irresistibly fascinated, Kierkegaard discerns Abraham's holiness to rest on a paradox, namely, his preparedness to stand above the Law out of respect for the Lawgiver. While it is incumbent upon every man qua father to love his own son, Abraham acknowledges a duty toward God which in effect contradicts his family obligations, let alone his natural impulses. He makes himself an exception to the universal, an offender against established public opinion, by obeying an esoteric supernatural voice enjoining murder. Thus Abraham is tempted by the ethical. Undoubtedly his unwillingness to sacrifice Isaac would have gained for him the approbation of everyone; but, acting against the inner light of *human* conscience and the ruling ideas of the crowd, Abraham became holy by "virtue of the absurd." Surely no contemporary could understand him except God.

Nothing is more offensive to the rationalist mind than exceptions to the rule. In the ideal world of the Enlightenment, justice shines as universally and unmistakably as the glory of Newton's laws. Hence it seems no mere accident of genius that Kierkegaard singled out this archaic Biblical myth for composing a "dialectic lyric" that calls into question the integrity of those who clearly have justice on their side. The Age of Reason and Sentiment was not receptive to mysterious voices telling an individual how to behave or what not to do unless they were audible to everyone. A man seduced by the dictates of his conscience, in opposition to the will of God, would have promptly been consigned to the madhouse by Dr. Johnson, although it must be admitted that perhaps he alone among his immediate contemporaries was sensitive to such an eventuality. The rise of pantheism with its absence of a sense of the "wholly other," the uniformity of nature, and the growing conviction that man's point of view (because that is the only one he ever truly knows) is decisive in all matters combined to render Kierkegaard's account *unzeitgemässig* (untimely). Even today, Biblical scholars often appear satisfied with viewing the Abraham story as an early protest against human sacrifice, as if Kierkegaard was bound to pedantic expositions of the obvious.

Kierkegaard's interpretation of the Abraham story in *Fear and Trembling* grows out of his protest against modes of thought and existence which Shakespeare had already condemned in *Measure for Measure*. At the beginning of the nineteenth century he specifically directed this protest, first, against Kant's ethical monism, his *Religion within the Bounds of Reason*, with its explicit denial of all autonomous religious value and its apotheosis of moral law to the neglect of grace; second, against the metaphysics of Romanticism with its veneration of experience, its subordination of responsibility to mood, and its sanction of seduction (lawlessness) in the name of freedom from convention; and, finally, against the more and more anthropocentric theism of the middle classes, who sought salvation from sin in unmolested respectability, and redemption in the cultivation of higher pleasures. The ideal self-sufficiency of Kant's moral agent, the Romantic hero's unawareness of his limitations, and the good Hegelian's adjustment to his historical epoch represent major alternatives to Christianity which Kierkegaard felt called upon to criticize for the sake of honesty.

The moral law being holy, Kant does not allow the moral agent to be answerable to God in a way that could conflict with his obligations toward other rational beings. In *Streit der Fakultäten* (Battle of the Faculties) he declares with regard to Abraham that the voice of God cannot be known save negatively as that not incongruous with the categorical imperative. However "majestic," he argues, man construes his confrontation by God to be, it becomes illusory by virtue of violating practical reason. Abraham, accordingly, should have answered God as follows: "That I ought not to kill my good son is certain beyond a shadow of a doubt; that you, as you appear to be, are God, I am not convinced and will never be even if your voice would resound from the (visible) heavens." [2]

Apart from his rationalistic conception of religious experience, Kant as a moralist makes no allowances for any distinctive expression of individuality. The moral agent ought not make his decisions dependent upon outward circumstance, however coercive it may prove to be in a special situation. While obedience may manifest itself in different forms of conduct, it is significant, for instance, that Kant cannot bring himself to recognize the possibility of a responsible lie.[3] Extraordinary moral action, therefore, he would rule out on two principal grounds: first, because virtue is not merely universal but absolute in the sense of divine; second, because every deviation from this supreme principle is gratuitous by definition.

If Kant's moralistic interpretation of the life of commitment is one extreme against which Kierkegaard reacted, Romantic individualism with its idolization of pursuit or mere becoming comprises the other. While Goethe's Faust, perhaps the most typical of Romantic heroes, violates the moral law out of an idealistic but insatiable desire to gain experience (leaving various ruined souls in his path), Laclos's Vicomte de Valmont, a distinguished predecessor, applying the scientific method to the art of seduction, enjoys a succession of "eternal moments," each of which in retrospect appears boring and disgusting. To be sure—like Lenau's Don Juan vainly in pursuit of ideal femininity, or Stendhal's Julien Sorel trying to make something of himself, or his virtual double, the seducer in Kierkegaard's *Diary of the Seducer*—the Vicomte has liberated himself from the more limiting forms of eighteenth-century conduct. He is prepared to take a risk in affirming himself over against the unimaginative compliance of his neighbors. Notwithstanding the intensity of his striving, it would seem to be the case that he and his like-minded relations never discovered themselves ultimately responsible to anything transcending their precious inwardness. Most Romantic heroes are seducers if not in the literal then in the figurative sense of the term; that is to say, they suspend the ethical because they feel constitutionally disposed to do so, not because they suddenly humble themselves before a higher power. Their intimations of immortality and eternal youth, in spite of indicating a degree of self-abandonment Diderot would have frowned upon as "religious," rarely (Byron is a notable exception) commit them to self-sacrificing action. Their unattainable wishes and daemonic dreams, their longing for tranquility and fear of boredom, their *Weltschmerz* and opportunistic piety (*Scheinheiligkeit*), represent a synthesis of aesthetic sensitivity and bewildered earnestness symptomatic of modern man's search for meaning. But Kierkergaard's Biblical category of the ethical-religious is as far removed from Faust's unrepentant striving as it is unlike the autonomy of Kant's moral agent.

Besides opposing the "poetical" and "puritanical" visions

of human destiny, Kierkegaard took issue with the sense of propriety and security permeating the novels of Jane Austen. The celebrated opening sentence of *Pride and Prejudice*—"It is a truth universally acknowledged that a single man in possession of a good fortune must be in want of a wife"—bespeaks a trust in impersonal providence Kierkegaard hated with all his heart and all his mind. This is bourgeois man calculating his future over teacups and biscuits, impervious to any unplanned interference with his aspirations. In *Fear and Trembling* Kierkegaard relates how a pastor in Copenhagen angrily tried to dissuade one of his parishioners from taking the Abraham story too much to heart. Without wishing to cast any aspersions on the effectiveness of his sermon, he must nevertheless insist that in the nineteenth century fathers no longer sacrifice their sons, however edifying the imitation of Abraham may appear on Sunday mornings. Hegel would have been very sympathetic towards this particular clergyman. Keenly aware of the dialectic evolution of Christian love, the great German philosopher prided himself on penetrating the rational depths of Biblical religion and making these real to his enlightened readers. Thus he speaks of Abraham:

> Love alone was beyond his power; even the one love he had, the love for his son, even his hope for posterity—the one mode of extending his being, the one mode of immortality he knew and hoped for—could depress him, trouble his all-exclusive heart and disquiet to such an extent that even this love he once wished to destroy; and his heart was quieted only through the certainty of the feeling that his love was not so strong as to render him unable to slay his beloved son with his own hand.[4]

Abraham's lack of love was *aufgehoben* (preserved and transformed) through New Testament love, which in turn culminated in the rise of culture.

Kierkegaard's confrontation of Christendom with a figure such as Abraham was an affront both to its aesthetic sensibilities and to its ethical self-righteousness. Where the humanists in their zeal for reform appealed to the conscience of mankind, here is a man whose own conscience was fallible in a particular situation; where the Romantics sought experience for experience's sake, here is a man who acted in fear and trembling lest he offend God; and where the middle-class Christian had ruled the daemonic out of court, here is a man who gains holiness precisely by breaking with routine, taking a risk, and venturing into the unanticipated against the grain. No wonder that Ibsen, Melville, and Dostoevsky, who, like Kierkegaard, were aroused by the hollowness of the various post-Enlightenment substitutes for genuine religion, should seize upon the "teleological suspension of the ethical" as a common theme in coming to terms with secular humanism. For when an individual is challenged to deviate from a norm whose ethicality is self-evident both to himself and to public opinion by "evidence of things unseen," he cannot justify himself by an appeal to scientific open-mindedness or world-historical necessity, or to fundamental decency. The props that up to this moment have sustained him through thick and thin no longer suffice, so that in his soul-searching he stands exposed to the unfathomable depth of being. As a result of doubting the dictates of his conscience, he experiences the apprehension of nonbeing and discovers himself, in Pascal's language, faced with the choice of overcoming his anxiety by approximating either a beast or an angel. Only the acknowledgment of man's dual nature (between heaven and hell) renders the "teleological suspension of the ethical" a meaningful alternative. Such eminent writers of the nineteenth century as Hawthorne and Melville in America, Dostoevsky and Tolstoy in Russia, Ibsen and Strindberg in Scandinavia, redirected attention to the ambiguity and paradox of being human. This enabled them to deal with the kind of issues the Encyclopedists had deemed obsolete.

Although, as Kierkegaard was careful to point out, Abraham remains a solitary "knight of faith," since he had no possible way of making his conduct intelligible even to his next of kin, his "borderline situation" raises questions that shed light on the loneliness, anxiety, hope, and temptation of all those whom Providence has not singled out for adjustment to a passing phase of history. While Sonia in *Crime and Punishment* can tell her friends that she took to the streets in order to save her family from starvation, she is, like Abraham, subject to being misunderstood. Billy Budd, about to ascend, blesses Captain Vere; like Abraham, he is making himself an exception to the class of murderers. Brand, with the *apatheia* and pride characteristic of Stoicism, completely disregards the feelings of his family in doing the apparent Will of God; like Sarah and Isaac, Agnes and Alf have every reason to question the sanity of their *pater familias*. Indeed, the problem of distinguishing daemonic possession from divine inspiration is as acute for those who become involved in a certain situation through no choice of their own as for those who are directly accountable for their conduct.

On what basis is one choice deserving of approbation as against another that should be judged unworthy or unreasonable? This issue seems particularly unresolvable when posed in terms of the "teleological suspension of the ethical." For then, compelled to re-examine our usual criteria, however germane to man's nature qua universal man, we must ask: In which respects is one course of action embraced "by virtue of the absurd" right and good, whereas the adoption of an alternative equally mad would constitute a violation of the ethical, not in the name of a superior value, but in that of the devil feigning the grandeur of God? Evidently sincerity must be recognized as a necessary condition for all responsible action. The presence of such an attitude is far from unmistakable; a man may be sincerely mistaken in pursuing a special goal. Thus a devout Nazi could argue that in supporting Hitler he was only incidentally furthering his personal interests inasmuch as he saw in the German leader an embodiment of new ultimate significance that he had hoped would help overcome the nihilism prevailing in the Western world today. As soon as one admits with Kierkegaard that "subjective truth" has its reasons that reason alone cannot comprehend, a mere appeal to the intellect is beside the point. Given a world in which God is "wholly other," where the real is not necessarily the rational, there does not appear any obvious way of telling whether someone or something is living proof of the infinite. Job's suffering, for example, was as much a mystery to himself as to his friends.

"It is great to give up one's wish," as Abraham did when he set out for Mount Moriah with Isaac, "but it is greater to hold it fast after having given it up," as he continued to believe in getting Isaac back. "It is great," Kierkegaard continues, "to grasp the eternal"—in other words, to act in accordance with the dictates of other-worldliness in spite of the pressures of outward circumstance—"but it is greater to hold fast to the temporal after having given it up," not to despair of the kingdom of heaven on earth even while living under the aspect of eternity.[5] Had Abraham tried to kill God instead of obeying him, he would have lacked resignation, the capacity to act contrary to impulse. On the other hand, had he despaired of getting Isaac back, he would have lacked faith, the capacity to believe in the possibility of the impossible. Analogously, Sonia at the most miserable moment of their lives affirmed the goodness of being in Raskolnikov's presence, and Billy Budd blessed Captain Vere under circumstances that would have kindled hatred and bitterness in most mortals. Not only did these individuals accept whatever happened to them without rebelliousness, but at the same time they refrained from indulging in the cynicism of unrequited virtue. Their exceptional behavior was attended by the following factors: spontaneous submission to necessity, heroic endurance of misfortune without subsequent disintegration, and an over-all awareness of the precariousness of finitude. It is evident that Billy Budd and Sonia were in harmony both with themselves and the world in such a way that they feared and trembled only before God. To be sure, this did not prevent them from acting contrary to the canons of respectability, as Abraham had also done.

Ibsen's Brand refuses to see his mother on her death-bed, neglects saving the life of his son Alf when he might have done so, contributes directly to the death of his wife Agnes, and leads his neighbors on a reckless crusade— all in the name of God, a God whom he could only imagine in the light of uncongenial justice. As if Christ had not suffered and died like a human being, Brand cannot reconcile himself to the paradox of absolute perfection radiating love in a sinful world. Thus, for the glory of God, he finds it necessary to become daemonically intolerant of human frailty. He grounds his contempt for pain and sorrow, as the majority of men experience these, in a view of humanity as totally unworthy of Christ's sacrifice. The ugliness of sin, he thinks, is sufficient reason for suspending his obligations towards the essentially human. His identification of affection and understanding with weakness and sentimentality leads him to assume a self-righteous disdain of imperfection. For Brand there is no middle ground between holiness and nothingness. In creating him, Ibsen personified the Kierkegaardian "Or" to the exclusion rather than the dethronement of the "Either."

Whereas Socrates, though annoyed by Xanthippe's tears, spends a good deal of his remaining mortal time comforting her, Brand is unable to bring himself to suppose that God might not be offended if a son should fulfil the last wish of an erring mother. On the verge of dying, she clings inordinately, he feels, to her few possessions. The kind of New Testament otherworldliness Brand vainly seeks to implant in his mother's heart before condescending to visit her is, ironically enough, a work of grace. Warned by a physician that his son will die unless the family moves away to a warmer climate for a while, he stays, suspecting that any alternate course of action would betray unwarranted weakness. A soldier of God who is not merely "wholly other" but, analogous to the Epicurean deities, beyond existence altogether, he cannot deviate from the path of duty for "private" reasons. His wife submits, and after the death of their son he condemns her memories of motherhood as sacrilegious, inasmuch as they conflict with the Will of God, who creates and destroys life as he pleases. When on one occasion Brand urges Agnes to give away not some but all of Alf's former clothing to a beggar, his demand must be interpreted as ethically dae-monic. It is not surprising that soon thereafter she dies also.

Entirely relieved of family responsibility, owing to con-ditions he found incommensurable with preaching the Gospel, Brand turns his attention to the construction of a new church. But once this desirable edifice is fact—like a Romantic shunning the reality that delighted him in anticipation—he turns his back upon it by choosing the day of consecration to launch an "attack upon Christen-dom." At first he succeeds in arousing the conscience of the burghers who see in him the possibility of a new life. But, having left the amenities of civilized existence behind them (including Brand's new church, which *he* had especially deprecated) in order to lead a disciple's life of constant uprootedness, it dawns on them that they may be confusing genuine Schleiermacherian *Jenseitsdrang* (spiritual striving) with *Wanderlust*. Moreover, exposed to hardships for which they were both physically and mentally unprepared, the crowd repudiates their prophet of a brief, ecstatic interval. Beguiled by false promises of quick material gain, they return to the security of home, but not before showering Brand with scorn and rocks. He is left to his own devices in midwinter and dies an outcast from the community he had hoped to reform. Just prior to being buried alive in an avalanche, a voice replies to his cry of despair: "God is *deus caritatis.*"

No doubt Brand's militant attitude toward sin in general and his appraisal of modern Christendom in particular were warranted by an intimate familiarity with certain passages in the Bible. Nevertheless, this insight blinded him to a more inclusive view of the human situation. If, as Plato suggests in the *Symposium* and Pascal in his *Pensées,* man occupies an intermediate position between being and nonbeing, guided, on the one hand, by love of perfection toward which he aspires, and, on the other, ever prey to the forces of chaos which threaten to destroy his spirituality, he does not deserve to be regarded as the incarnation either of pure negativity or—as the humanists would advocate—of potential self-sufficiency. From Brand's perspective it would be hard to distinguish the devil in the human community. He cannot love his neighbor in spite of his sins because for him the double-mindedness of human beings entails their complete worthlessness before God. He seems aesthetically offended as well as ethically outraged by the untidiness of our mortal lot. Where (through the power of Mozartean realism) Don Giovanni emerges as a likable figure notwithstanding his daemonic capacity for plunging into immediate experience, Brand would have cut him off from grace altogether. He was unrealistic in losing sight of the double nature of man involved in all the contradictions of infinite longing at variance with finite limitations; he was un-Christian because the task of a Christian is to love rather than to judge. Even the individual who is uniquely answerable to God at a certain moment in history remains, by virtue of his nature, a fallible being. He, more than the ordinary mortal, must fear and tremble, for, the closer a man has come to God, the greater his sin against the Holy Ghost in violating the trust.

When, as in Brand's case, the ethical stage on life's way is first confused with the religious and then suspended, the actions which spring from such a commitment are fanatic, to say the least. The single-mindedness with which he pursues righteousness to the exclusion of charity, while religiously motivated, comprises as much a violation of God's love for man as Don Giovanni's aesthetically motivated pursuit of women or the Grand Inquisitor's ecclesiastically inspired persecution of the founder of his religion. While the Don lusts after the repetition of immediacy and the Grand Inquisitor after indestructible finite authority, Brand is seduced by righteousness. Self-appointed guardian of God's ways, he appears, in dealing with his neighbor, unable to think through or feel the pathos of being human. He is deficient in what Kierkegaard has called the humor of the religious man, who comes to terms with the discrepancy between deeds and professed beliefs prevailing in this world, not through righteous indignation or cynical indifference, but instead through awareness of man's frailty and dependence on others. Unlike Brand, the religious man is free to laugh occasionally at his own pretensions and weaknesses.

Brand's apparent "teleological suspension of the ethical" is not a suspension of this kind at all, but, to the extent that his Either/Or excludes the possibility of unmerited grace, the hypostatization of a single attribute of God. Consonant with Kant's moral agent, Brand has successfully subordinated drives for private gain and pleasure to obedience, but—and this precisely is an eventuality Kant envisaged with approbation—in doing so, he became the tool of his own principles. As Kant's moral agent ought not to tell a lie even where it might prevent a murder, so Brand feels obligated to watch various members of his family die because, he reasons, a servant of God has no right to be charitable. His consistency in overlooking the specific character of each situation that confronts him with the need of decision (so unlike Jesus) is frightening. Not until the very end is his self-assurance undermined to a degree where he can begin doubting himself. Previously he acted with the prerogative of God himself, unmindful of being mistaken. Of course, from a Kantian point of view, he is subject to praise for controlling again and again the desires of his natural self. He did not enjoy inflicting pain on those closest to his heart. Had Abraham not been ethical, his temporary suspension of the ethical would be trivial; by the same token, had Brand not been *religiously ethical*, his unwillingness to become *ethical-religious* would have no special significance. It is the very sincerity with which he conceives the Will of God as manifest in justice alone that lends tragic depth to his disintegration. Indeed, Ibsen's Brand confirms Dr. Johnson's famous saying: "The road to hell is paved with good intentions." Duty without love can be as destructive as spontaneity devoid of dedication.

Captain Vere and Billy Budd are concrete embodiments of the ethical and religious ways of being in the truth, as Kierkegaard differentiates the two. Both act in accordance with their respective knowledge of the good; but where the Captain is unwilling to deviate from the highest ethics of conformity, Budd, in his unstudied manner, takes a stand above the law. Nowhere else in American literature is there a more convincing exploration of the issue raised by Kierkegaard in *Fear and Trembling*. The antagonists suddenly find themselves in a situation that reveals their relationship to themselves, to each other, and to the ultimate ground of being. The unfolding of events puts to a test their deepest commitments: Billy Budd, guileless and innocent in contrast to the large majority of men, is sadistically provoked by Claggart to transgress the law and murder him in a fit of impetuous passion. Captain Vere, a sensitive but conscientious disciplinarian, enforces naval law and has Billy Budd hanged. At the same time he is disquieted by his judgment of Budd's basic innocence over against Claggart's ill-concealed malice. But he insists that morality must not be suspended at sea, especially when there is real danger that one exception to the rule might touch off a general rebellion. Just as the pastor in Copenhagen feared for the worldly order if fathers should begin imitating Abraham, what would happen to it, wonders Captain Vere, if the crew of the *Indomitable* beheld an unpunished seaman in its midst?

Melville allows that "the monkish devotee of military duty . . . may in the end have caught Billy to his arms as Abraham may have caught young Isaac on the brink of resolutely offering him up in obedience to the exacting demand." But, as far as the world was concerned, Vere maintained "a stoic exterior," forbearing indulgence in such paternal emotions. Even the Chaplain, "having been made acquainted with the young sailor's essential innocence," did not actively intercede in his behalf. To be sure, he dispensed with the ceremonial use of ecclesiastical language as he conferred on him a final kiss, an act of recognition which might conceivably have led to saving Billy's life. Perhaps circumstances were too coercive for this to be permitted to happen. Certainly Vere, instead of translating the dictates of his conscience into some appropriate steps testifying to their presence, chose the *status quo* as his ultimate effectual criterion. Few men, admittedly, would have done otherwise; nevertheless, this does not justify his halfhearted adherence to a double standard of conduct. Budd, the likable sailor, is sacrificed for being a defective link in an impersonal chain known as the fleet. Are there not times to be unpatriotic in the name of more universal values? In our time this question is raised in almost every discussion of the behavior of Hitler's officers during the Second World War.

A religious element does not directly enter into the situation until Billy, ascending, remarks to the startled witnesses of his destiny: "God bless Captain Vere." Prior to this unique pronouncement, his predicament had called into question the relationship between legality and ethicality; now it focuses attention on the extramundane. God bless the Captain, who knew in his heart what he ought to do, who was genuinely concerned about being in the truth, but who could not compel himself to make the movement from possibility to actuality. Billy Budd submits to his lot without casting aspersions on the integrity of the man in whose power it lay to save his life. By blessing Captain Vere, he realizes in fact what the Captain could only grasp in theory: that the categories of legality, as it were, are inadequate to render a fair account of what in fact *is* the case in a problematical context.

Whereas Vere may be said to have acted in accordance with Aristotle's ethics, good-naturedly and after careful deliberation, Billy Budd, touched by the Christian folly, prays for the salvation of his executioner. His behavior is properly assessed as unnatural, dangerous to a well-functioning ship; and it is with this threat in mind that subsequent to the execution the officers do their hurried utmost to create an illusion of normality, as if nothing out of the ordinary had just transpired. Ironically enough, Captain Vere, in refusing to follow the dictates of his conscience, was afraid of the very thing Budd's last freely uttered words accomplished in an instant. For the Captain had reasoned that to place himself above naval law by endorsing Budd's acquittal would jeopardize the "animal faith" sailors are supposed to have regarding necessary connections between certain matters of fact. But this was precisely the effect of Billy's benediction. Is it any less "unusual" for a foretopman to imitate Christ than for a captain to act like a human being? When all was said and done, there was general if not universal agreement on Billy Budd's innocence, his story, Melville tells us, assuming the character of myth for sailors around the world. Against a background of dissension in the British navy at that time, reports of Billy Budd's martyrdom cannot but have undermined the morale Captain Vere had been so anxious to sustain.

What infuriated Claggart and puzzled everyone who came in contact with Billy was his being in a state of grace. Although handicapped by a speech impediment, which served as a condition for his recourse to physical violence during the crucial interview with Claggart, this lapse belied what Melville refers to as the supernatural origin of his character and physical beauty. The fundamental purity of his disposition sets him apart from the rest of the officers and crew as soon as he is constrained to join the *Indomitable*. Not only Claggart, who has a stake in destroying what he dare not hope to possess, but the others also feel themselves in the presence of a qualitatively exceptional individual. At first they tend to look upon his single-mindedness and directness as indicative of deficient virility. A seaman, they instinctively postulate, who is seized to serve against his will must bemoan his fate and curse his abductors. Billy Budd, by remaining himself, gains their wonder and incurs their wrath. Gradually he even gains their respect. It is this more than anything else that agitates Claggart, who finds the buoyancy and warmth of unshakable integrity a foil to his vanity. Captain Vere, though favorably impressed by Billy's deportment, does not understand him either. Accustomed, as most high-minded men of experience are wont to be, to observing good in a Manichean conflict with evil (the presupposition of the ethical per ethical), he cannot fathom the nature of Christ-like goodness. The man for whom Captain Vere would not suspend the ethical was already beyond the ethical—in a state of grace. Only the blessed bless their enemies.

Raskolnikov's murder of the pawnwoman and her sister, Lizaveta, while immediately motivated by hunger, poverty, and a sense of guilt arising from unfulfilled family obligations, was at the same time grounded in a theory of human nature to which he had not altogether facetiously subscribed. According to this view, mankind is roughly divisible into two classes: the ordinary and the extraordinary. The former are naturally destined to obey the laws of their society, while the latter, by virture of constitutional superiority, have the right to transgress them in the name of progress.[6] They constitute the independent men, the geniuses of the race whose growth has not been stunted by habit, tradition, and fear of authority. Revolutions, so argues Raskolnikov, are invariably initiated by those courageous enough to overstep generally accepted limits in an act of defiance which the *hoi polloi* label as criminal. A Napoleon must place himself above ordinary sanctions in order to confer hitherto unknown benefits on humanity. He may be said to be tempted by the ethical insofar as doing his duty in the customary sense of responsible action would entail a negation of his historical mission. After Hegel's Owl of Minerva has spoken, he represents one of history's great figures.

Since Raskolnikov regarded the pawnwoman merely as an incidental nuisance to society—she was, in fact, quite disagreeable—he came to conceive her existence as superfluous. She thwarted his highest aspirations. Raskolnikov needed money desperately in order to dissuade his sister from teleologically suspending the ethical in her own case by entering into a marriage of convenience for her brother's sake, and to tide over his mother until better days. Although he would not tolerate the idea of Dounia's sacrifice, her suitor being an arrogant but affluent businessman with connections, on his own he was prepared to act contrary to justice. Not that he was carried away by illusions of grandeur; but, to the degree that his personal circumstances warranted radical change, he believed the end to justify the means. Until Lizaveta became an unexpected witness to the crime, he had never entertained the hypothesis of a double killing. A kind of Nietzschean Romanticism ingrained in his character could not be satisfied by anything less than perfection. Thus Lizaveta was also murdered.[7]

In spite of the fact that Raskolnikov could not really attribute any world-historical importance to his own exceptional conduct, his theory of it was influenced by various corresponding creeds under attack in *Crime and Punishment*: Carlyle's (Hegelian) veneration of pragmatic greatness, Flaubert's divinely appointed artist, Marx's idealization of proletarian human nature, Nietzsche's autonomous aristocrat of impulse—each of these distinctively exemplifies the disregard of limitations and the assumption of peculiar rights characteristic of late Romanticism. Throughout his works Dostoevsky was intent on elucidating the implications of his belief, abhorrent to liberal humanism, that without God everything is permitted to man. Raskolnikov made himself the arbiter of his own destiny. His failure to acknowledge any extra-mundane authority transcending the transitory values of individuality and society is symptomatic of the breakdown of commitments at the end of the nineteenth century. Up to the time of his conversion in a Siberian prison camp, Raskolnikov's attitude toward himself and the world around him is prophetically contemporaneous—cynical, disillusioned, and indifferent. Combined with his passion for feverish activity, it threatens to destroy him. Certainly there is a close resemblance between Raskolnikov's godlessness and the disintegration of intellectuals, political agitators, and artists, which never ceased to fascinate Dostoevsky in examining their pseudo religions.

Having duplicated in action what appeared warranted in examination, Raskolnikov broke down. The extraordinary individual of his theory notwithstanding, he suffers pangs of conscience. His need to confess his crime, his return to its scene, and his constant trepidation are incongruous with the perseverance of a dedicated idealist. When his mother and sister arrive to visit their favorite, they find him unhinged. By itself Raskolnikov's failure to keep his nerve offers no refutation of his theory. Where he failed, someone else might have succeeded. At first he mulls over his execution of the crime without questioning the daemon of its designer. From his initial pragmatic standpoint the crucial issue becomes whether he bungled the job. An inquiry into the self that conceived the project must await his encounter with Sonia. As Kierkegaard insists over and over, a man will only despair or rejoice over issues germane to his particular way of being in the truth. Hence Raskolnikov is in no position to see his predicament in the light of inwardness until he has experienced what it means to be separated from God. Aside from apparent success or failure, he must despair of worldliness before he can conquer his terror of the world.

After Dounia, Raskolnikov's sister, has disclosed her willingness to marry the undesirable Luzhin, her brother rejects this plan by challenging her to choose between himself and this marriage. Actually Dounia had given no explicit indication of wishing to sacrifice herself for her family. Raskolnikov—in this case well guided by intuition —despised him from the start. Dounia resented being confronted by an Either/Or which, although drawn up in her interest, was rather inconsiderate of her feelings. Her devotion to her brother, after all, never had exclusive claim on her choices even with regard to Luzhin. However this may be, it is doubly ironic that Raskolnikov forbade his sister to act in a manner consonant with the disposition of the woman who became the instrument of his salvation. Dounia was prepared to do as much for her family as Sonia subsequently did for him; but of course he could not see matters thus when, full of "Schillerian enthusiasm," he remonstrated with her.

Like Raskolnikov, Sonia crossed the border between respectability and blessedness (or damnation). She went out on the streets to save her family from starvation. The selflessness of her love in the midst of circumstances that would have tried the faith of Job bespeaks an element of otherworldliness in her nature conspicuously absent from Raskolnikov's temerity and ruthlessness. A living refutation of Nietzsche's identification of strength with incessant drive, Sonia's capacity for suffering and forgiveness, as well as her glowing passivity, exemplifies religiousness at its best. Becoming a prostitute out of charity and accompanying a disgruntled and disgraced prisoner to Siberia can only perversely be interpreted as acts of weakness. At the same time she does these things so freely and single-mindedly that a bystander might infer she had no will of her own. But this precisely is the paradox of agape: the individual loses his will in order to do the will of God. In contrast to Raskolnikov, who contemplates suicide as a means of evading his conscience, Sonia's one concern is to help those who need help most. The completion of life in time does not grip her with anxiety. Unconcerned with the pursuit of external advantage, she has found her vocation in comforting suffering humanity. She is free from Brand's and Raskolnikov's presumption that man qua man can ever be absolutely certain or independent.

Through her, Raskolnikov discovers that in the eyes of God no human being is without worth, that the outcome of an enterprise is no reliable clue to its value, and that thought divorced from empathy is corrupting. While he thinks, judges, and broods, Sonia loves, sustains, and hopes. Faith in the overruling goodness of God enables her to deal with the most terrible calamities without falling into despair. Whatever happens to her in the world cannot undermine this faith. From their first meeting Raskolnikov suspects that she alone can reconcile him to himself. Her endurance of the suffering that he intentionally inflicts upon her—because like the Underground Man in the presence of Liza, he is put to shame by her purity—intensifies his longing to be with her. But Sonia, who is as intimately aware of suffering as Raskolnikov, does not allow sensitivity to interfere with her redemptive mission. When she induces him freely to choose exile, he at first hesitates to accept the consequences of such a decision. His confession precedes his conversion, which true to the New Testament, is described as a moment of intense illumination:

How it happened he did not know, but suddenly something seemed to seize him and throw him at [Sonia's] feet. He embraced her knees and wept. At first she was terribly frightened, and her face was covered by a deathly pallor. She jumped to her feet and trembling all over, looked at him. But at one and the same moment she understood everything. Her eyes shone with intense happiness; she understood, and she had no doubts at all about it, that he loved her, loved her infinitely, and that the moment she had waited for so long had come at last.[8]

Raskolnikov the murderer was saved by grace mediated through Sonia the prostitute. But her transgression of the law, unlike his, was a work of love. If this was the only way in which she could allay the desperate anxiety of some fellow creature, then it became her duty to adopt it. There was no theory at stake in her action, no self-conscious comparison with historical or fictional characters. Raskolnikov wonders how many respectable murderers and adulterers are at legal liberty because they lack the courage to affirm themselves in accordance with their "infinite passion." Christ's Sermon on the Mount notwithstanding, society continues to make a basic distinction between committing adultery in one's heart and in one's neighbor's house. While, from a practical point of view, this is indispensable, the public conscience is always prone to confound manifestations of grace with those of outrageousness, both resembling inequities within an ordered scheme. Had Sonia had occasion to sacrifice someone else's life rather than her own, she might, being Sonia, have been justified. Raskolnikov had to experience the "shaking of the foundations" in order to discover God. He was sent to Siberia by representatives of law and order; but his redemption was effected by a woman who had herself become an outcast from society. She, too, in the Christian sense, stood above good and evil; for God had blessed her.[9]

CHAPTER VII

The Breakdown of Romantic Enlightenment:
Kafka and Dehumanization

The question is not to paint something altogether different from a man, a house, a mountain, but to paint a man who resembles a man as little as possible; a house that preserves of a house exactly what is needed to reveal a metamorphosis; a cone miraculously emerging—as the snake from his slough—from what used to be a mountain. For the modern artist, aesthetic pleasure derives from such a triumph over human matter. That is why he has to drive home the victory by presenting in each case the strangled victim.

Ortega y Gasset[1]

Like other honest haters of surface Christianity, Kierkegaard is open to the charge of being the devil's advocate—a daemonic possibility that no doubt he entertained himself. In accentuating the difficulties of becoming a Christian in Christendom he could scarcely help providing the enemies of theism with valuable weapons for their own cause. *Training in Christianity* conveniently lends itself to a vindication of atheism, if the arguments enumerated therein for not espousing the faith are transposed from their intended Biblical orientation to a scientific-naturalistic framework. Irrespective of Kierkegaard's own final position, his method of "indirect communication" proves double-edged. After Pascal no serious apologist for Christianity could avoid coming to terms with the religious hostility or indifference of the emancipated intellectual, and it attests to no little part of his greatness that Kierkegaard eventually succeeded in rousing this intellectual's attention. As it turned out, he might well have thought that this happened for the wrong reasons. Nevertheless, his dialectical irony has become the measure of Christendom.

Whether or not Kafka was a genuine Kierkegaardian, there is no question that the study of Kierkegaard made a profound impression upon him. Moreover, apart from this direct influence, Kafka's authorship shows remarkable resemblances to Kierkegaard's which are no less significant for being inadvertent. Nor is it especially fruitful in this connection to dwell on their common fear of the male parent and related psychoanalytic correspondences. Far more intriguing (at least for the historian of ideas) than their personalities is their work, and it is here that their legacy must be traced. Very much like Kierkegaard, Kafka has been subjected to every conceivable interpretation. Some find his stories full of humor, others grotesque; some see him as a champion of Zionism, others as a nihilist par excellence. His preoccupation with dream imagery has kept the Freudians happy while his "symbolism" remains grist for the mill of the new critics. Could a true nihilist describe nihilism? In this confusing situation it may not be amiss to analyze four of Kafka's stories through Kierkegaardian categories in order to suggest how they illuminate the breakdown of Romantic Enlightenment.

The stories are: "Metamorphosis," "The Penal Colony," "The Hunger Artist," and "The Burrow." [2] Their respective heroes: a commercial traveler, an army officer, a hunger artist, and, though Kafka only speaks of "he," a mole. Each, in Kierkegaardian terms, is a "solitary individual." Gregor Samsa, the commerical traveler, is isolated from his family, who make no effort to understand him although he is prepared to sacrifice himself for their sake. The officer in a state of neurotic self-absorption carries on the tradition of "exquisite torture" of the Old Commandant, in opposition to the new regime, which favors other methods of realizing justice. It is the officer's loneliness, his failure to persuade the visiting explorer of the righteousness of his cause, that leads him to execute himself. The hunger artist, too, is alone. His public enjoys his performances for the wrong reasons; moreover, it persists in thinking that he aims to hoodwink people. Only the children "showed by the brightness of their intent eyes that new and better times might be coming." [3] Finally, the mole devotes every ounce of his energy to shunning the world.

The *philosophes* gathering in their *salons* took delight in the interchange of wit and worldly wisdom. The Romantics made a cult of friendship, often wearing their hearts on their sleeves as they commiserated over the tragedy of life. Socialists prefer to organize heaven on earth and physicists are bound together by laboratory objectivity. Contemporary man seeks invulnerability, and, if sensitive, is perhaps overly worried about dying of soullessness.

Next to a shared state of estrangement the outstanding feature of these four beings is their repulsiveness, or, as Kierkegaard might have put it, their "wholly otherness." By virtue of his metamorphosis Gregor Samsa is transformed into an insect, but a self-conscious insect—a roach's body equipped with a human mind. The grotesqueness of his story is accounted for in large measure by the uneasy union of these two sets of characteristics. Gregor can follow the drift of his family's conversation whereas for them he has become a mere commodity. Though Kafka contrasts Gregor's unyielding kindliness with their ever-increasing callousness, the reader should ask himself how he would act if a close friend or relative suddenly were to assume animal shape. The officer is a depraved humanist who operates his instrument of torture with reasoning intellect and great skill. His sadism is enhanced by aesthetic refinement. He would not be satisfied with plain murder or even genocide. What fascinates him is the appropriate process by which the condemned prisoner pays for his guilt. The same discipline and control that a humanist brings to the task of self-realization, the officer applies to breaking the human will.

The hunger artist represents a further inversion of *humanitas*. Why should a man who fasts professionally be called an artist? To be sure, art can be embodied in a way of life as well as in fixed works, but a way of life that is suicidally passive without bringing life to others seems a denial of creativity. A related denial occurs in "The Burrow," where the mole is compulsively driven to ward off real, or, more likely, imaginary enemies. Its mastery of method is indeed worthy of the finest engineer, but without fruitful consequences for anyone. "So I begin by shovelling the soil back into the holes from which it was taken, a kind of work that I am familiar with, that I have done countless times almost without regarding it as work, and at which, particularly as regards the final pressing and smoothing down—and this is no empty boast, but the simple truth—I am unbeatable." [4]

In the Enlightenment man was proud, possibly too much so, of walking on two legs and looking up into the sky. With Romanticism he entered more and more into himself. Schopenhauer renounced the world, Nietzsche set out to transform it in his own image, and there were many who went underground. Post-Darwinian man often delights in his kinship (*Gleichschaltung*) with the animal kingdom and likes to think of his nature as being uniform with nature at large. Rousseau's hopes have been realized beyond all expectation: man is back in the jungle, but alas! not the one Jean-Jacques dreamt of.

Gregor Samsa discovers a new kind of freedom as he hangs suspended from the ceiling (something he could not do before), though getting out of bed is far more arduous now. In view of the life of a commercial traveler caught in a bureaucratic system, it is doubtful whether Gregor was any freer then than after his metamorphosis. He never chose his occupation, it would appear, just as he never asked to become an insect. Always he is in the grip of forces outside of himself which determine his destiny. He remains at the mercy of his family, who long ago crushed—if not his love—his will to lead a life of his own. The officer is a slave to his idea of justice. Like a typical Dostoevskian hero, his humanity corrodes from the impact of free-floating intelligence. He illustrates the thesis that men are not necessarily free because they can think straight. But the hunger artist, as he lies dying, asserts his freedom only to eat the food he likes, and explains his passion for fasting by the lack of such. Kafka effectively contrasts this act of self-transcendence with the natural greed of the panther which, succeeding the hunger artist in the cage, scores a much bigger success. People enjoy watching its unstudied vitality where before they were offended by the unnaturalness of a happily starving man. They overlook the impossibility of a panther culture. Paradoxical as it may seem, a fasting person (behind bars) enjoys a far greater degree of freedom than a wild animal. On the other hand, the mole has no real freedom. Presumably his mode of life frees him from the world, but he cannot live with himself without anxiety. His burrow turns out to be more a prison than a refuge. From inside he cannot spot the potential enemy in wait above, and outside he has left the safety of the burrow.

After the French Revolution, naïveté about freedom should have disappeared. To the fact that it did not we owe much of nineteenth-century radicalism. With the notable exception of Kant, the Enlightenment conceived of freedom as absence of external constraint. Change circumstances and you change the individual and society. Dostoevsky and a few others saw through this dangerous oversimplification. Freud, in this respect like Christianity, sees man as fundamentally enslaved to himself. There can be no real freedom for sinners or neurotics regardless of what government they live under. Sartre and the existentialists have attempted to defend a more radical human freedom. The hunger artist, a Marxist critic might say, is being exploited by his middle-class public. If this be so, the fact remains that he is free while they are not.

Rather remarkably these four individuals of Kafka's imagination disclose themselves as moral beings. Gregor endures every calamity that befalls him. Nothing deters him from doing his duty by his family even after they have given unmistakable evidence of their contempt. From the very start of his metamorphosis he goes out of his way to spare them unnecessary bother or embarrassment. He is determined to work as usual, and having taken stock of his helplessness, never ceases to brood over the awkward position in which he has placed his financially dependent parents and sister. And, in his diabolical way, the officer reveals an exemplary dedication to his equipment. He is no practitioner of self-indulgence. On the contrary, he takes his job most seriously and in the end dies for his beliefs. When he puts himself under the harrow in place of the prisoner, *he* does not have to be bound. His sincerity is a moral virtue and he does have standards of his own. How many of the S.S. were willing to suffer voluntarily the fate they imposed on their victims? As regards the hunger artist, his uncompromising devotion to fasting sets him apart from all who come into contact with him. The overseer is merely interested in making money; the public is always looking for thrills between bouts of boredom; and the guards, ironically enough, can never catch the hunger artist cheating (if he were to cheat) because their endurance does not last twenty-four hours. Also conspicuously persevering is the mole in his burrow. He never gives up—in spite of the approaching enemy, the neurotic fears, and the multitude of obstacles in his path to perfect security. Like the organization man bent on getting to the top, he stops short of nothing to get to the bottom. With old age already upon him he sets to work again repairing the undermined foundations of his Castle Keep.

If Kierkegaard's *Either/Or* is interpreted as describing the life of indulgence or intoxication over against the life of patience or resignation, Kafka's heroes in these stories definitely lead the latter. Far from being seduced by the varieties of pleasure, they suffer from a lack of immediacy. In their rigid isolation they succumb to the temptation of the ethical. What better lesson in perverse commitment than Gregor's to his sister, the officer's to justice, the hunger artist's to more than forty days of fasting, and the mole's to digging his burrow. Concerning their situations it is pertinent to observe: if only the world had offered them some distraction such as a chance love affair, they might have spared themselves.

For large segments of Western society even today, immorality is identified with being in a state of disgrace, or with the loss of respectability. The typical immoralist in the fiction of the Romantic Enlightenment is the woman who has compromised her virtue or the man who has broken a promise. For the rationalist morality is rooted in principle. For the Romantic it resides in spontaneous emotion. The twentieth century has witnessed so many instances of sincere perversity and principled ruthlessness that the Romantic Enlightenment image of moral man is no longer adequate. Surely there is nothing disgraceful about an officer doing his duty, a hunger artist performing his act, a mole digging his burrow, and a commercial traveler dedicated to his employer and family. All of them are very loyal and unpretentious—the kind of beings secret societies like to attract for membership.

Each has a religious experience, a flash of revelation which stands out amidst his dreary methodical existence. For Kierkegaard an individual embraces the Christian faith "by virtue of the absurd." In short, there is no philosophical road to God. This element of absurdity will also be found in the following descriptions:

> Was [Gregor] an animal, that music had such an effect upon him? He felt as if the way were opening before him to the unknown nourishment he craved. He was determined to push forward till he reached his sister, to pull at her skirt and so let her know that she was to come into his room with her violin, for no one here appreciated her playing as he would appreciate it. He would never let her out of his room at least, not so long as he lived; his frightful appearance would become, for the first time, useful to him; he would watch all the doors of his room at once and spit at intruders; but his sister should need no constraint, she should stay with him of her own free will; she should sit beside him on the sofa, bend down her ear to him and hear him confide that he had had the firm intention of sending her to the Conservatorium, and that, but for his mishap, last Christmas—surely Christmas was long past?—he would have announced it to everybody without allowing a single objection. After this confession his sister would be so touched that she would burst into tears, and Gregor would then raise himself to her shoulder and kiss her on the neck, which, now that

she went to business, she kept free of any ribbon or collar.[5]

Well, and then came the sixth hour! It was impossible to grant all the requests to be allowed to watch it from near by. The Commandant in his wisdom ordained that the children should have the preference; I [the officer], of course, because of my office had the privilege of always being at hand; often enough I would be squatting there with a small child in either arm. How we all absorbed the look of transfiguration on the face of the sufferer, how we bathed our cheeks in the radiance of that justice, achieved at last and fading so quickly! What times these were, my comrade! [6]

"Because," said the hunger artist, lifting his head a little and speaking with his lips pursed, as if for a kiss, right into the overseer's ear, so that no syllable might be lost, "because I couldn't find the food I liked. If I had found it, believe me, I should have made no fuss and stuffed myself like you or anyone else." [7]

Also I am not permanently doomed to this free life, for I know that my term is measured, that I do not have to hunt here forever, and that, whenever I am weary of this life and wish to leave it, Someone, whose invitation I shall not be able to withstand, will, so to speak, summon me to him.[8]

Scene One: Gregor Samsa, now transformed into an insect, despised and neglected by his family for whom he worked himself to the bone, hears his sister play the violin. The Samsas are having their boarders in for a small get-together. These boarders had to be taken into the household to compensate for Gregor's missing wages. The family does everything to conceal the presence of their ungainly member, especially since they hold him responsible for their presently ambiguous respectability. Gregor finds his sister's playing ravishing. It arouses in him a stream of love and affection that temporarily eclipses his fate. Having already shown herself to him as ungrateful and selfish, Gregor has sufficient reason to spurn her. Instead he dreams of communicating his abiding love, and imagines himself listening entranced to her music-making. It is absurd. On the day of his death the Samsa family makes an excursion, having convinced themselves that they need a good rest. In fact, the discovery of Gregor lovingly inching himself up to his sister turned out to be the major contributing factor to his demise. The Samsas were horrified, not least on account of the boarders, who immediately threatened to leave. Mr. Samsa was able to save his pride only because he could give them notice the following morning after Gregor was found dead. Through all this meanness and pointlessness Gregor's integrity shines like a star. The goodness of his will hinges on no pragmatic formula. It transcends both justice and common sense.

Scene Two: "What the others had found in the machine the officer had not found" [9]—nevertheless, he had found it, vicariously. The "sixth hour" was the hour of Enlightenment. "Nothing more happens than that the man begins to understand the inscription, he purses his mouth as if he were listening. You may have seen how difficult it is to decipher the script with one's eyes; but our man deciphers it with his wounds." [10] The officer describes this moment as a revelatory experience reminiscent of the Crucifixion. What a sight! Here is the officer with a child in each arm absorbing transfiguration and bathing "in the radiance" of justice. Nothing is less edifying than an engineer experiencing bliss. With his fascination for design and orderly procedure it is incongruous seeing him participate in a mystical ecstasy. Thus the luminous quality of justice makes its claim upon him, and he is transported. Is this, Professor Richard Kroner once asked in a lecture, the only kind of reverence which still can grip modern man? The absurdity of it all is nauseating. Christ's suffering on the Cross was to redeem mankind. When he drew children to Him he was not in agony. In contrast, the prisoner's suffering seems senseless. He has become the victim of a daemonic, mechanical mentality, and the children are given first-row seats to view the proceedings. To experience the void may, of course, have a holiness of its own.

Scene Three: The hunger artist's affirmation to eat only the food he likes has a ring of childish spitefulness. At the same time it exemplifies the faith that sustains him through continuous fasting and the misapprehension of the crowd. What food is he looking for? The religious symbolism here is utterly convincing. Like Christ's stay in the wilderness, his official fast lasts forty days. Like Christ, who in resisting the devil replied that man does not live by bread alone, the hunger artist cannot be tempted by economic materialism. But the differences in these two situations are even more revealing than the resemblances. While Christ returned to the world following His forty days and nights of solitude, and whereas He did not repudiate ordinary bread but merely its idolatry—did He not break bread with His disciples?—the hunger artist persists in fasting as if driven by a death instinct, and, correlatively, he never finds any food worthy of man. He preserves his freedom above natural necessity, but what this freedom might be for is never made clear. This is a characteristic Kafkaesque inversion. For the mystic, fasting is a way toward spiritual illumination. Ascetic discipline serves to open up the soul to an immediately felt presence of the divine. The hunger artist, on the other hand, fasts for the sake of fasting, hence without achieving a comparable state of liberation. This makes his final utterance both sublime and absurd. His inviolate integrity suggests the perfection of a Stradivarius violin that for want of being played decays.

Scene Four: The mole's paradoxical confession of faith might well have come from the pages of Kierkegaard, particularly his expressions, "permanently doomed to this free life," and "Someone, whose invitation I shall not be able to withstand, will, so to speak, summon me to him." There is a corresponding chasm separating the mole in his burrow from the world and dividing the human from the divine. Just as man is doomed to pursue his own schemes oblivious of God's grace, the mole labors under the illusion of freedom in constructing his underground ivory tower. Yet he is dimly aware of the futility of his project, as the seemingly most self-sufficient person will doubt his autonomy in the face of death, suffering, and other evidence of finitude. There is a paradox here. The mole devotes his entire existence to warding off intrusions even though he realizes this to be an unrealizable aim. Similarly, hedonists strive for unperturbed happiness against the odds of existence. But at least the mole knows that this does not constitute the end of his destiny. Half-willingly ("whenever I am weary of this life"), half-unwillingly (by "invitation I shall not be able to withstand"), he yearns for salvation. Kierkegaard's "Wholly Other" (God) here becomes "Someone." This "Someone," as God does with obdurate sinners, will summon the mole to him. This guilt-ridden creature's redemption seems absurd, but really no more so than the promised purity of man before God at the end of time.

Kant had faith in the moral law within and the starry heavens above. No doubt this was the noblest expression of Enlightenment rationalism. The Romantics believed in nature, history, and art. Essentially they were Christian pantheists. Other ecstasies modern man has experienced include the Party, Science, Nation, Race, and Money. Little wonder that by the twentieth century there emerged a growing number of believers in nothing. But this is a contradiction. Man must believe in something. Consequently the believers in nothing, like prostitutes pretending love, have ecstasies of their own.

As matters evolve for Kafka's extraordinary creatures, despair rather than salvation is their final lot. Each dies a miserable death. Gregor Samsa bombarded by his father with apples, one of which hurts him grievously, and, worst of all, completely misunderstood, is found dead one morning by the cleaning woman. "What the others had found in the machine the officer had not found: the lips were firmly pressed together, the eyes were open, with the same expression as in life, the look was calm and convinced, through the forehead went the point of the great iron spike." [11] But the transfiguration of the sixth hour had eluded him, and that alone could have justified his faith. Like Gregor Samsa, the hunger artist dies an outcast from society. Not only is his a horrible end, but there is no evidence that it made any impression, even after his remarkable last words. Immediately on his demise a panther is substituted as the new attraction, with a conspicuous rise in spectator interest. And the mole never finds peace. In our last glimpse of him he is desperately devising defenses against the approaching beast whose fluctuating audibility and silence fills him with infinite anxiety: "Even if it should be such a peculiar beast as to be able to tolerate a neighbor near its burrow, it could not tolerate my burrow, it would not tolerate in any case a neighbor who could be clearly heard." [12]

Enlightenment thought was militantly Pelagian. The Romantics, though suffering from *Weltschmerz* and ennui, continued to sing of liberty and tear-stained joy. Contemporary man often has nothing left to say. The annihilation of Kafka's heroes is not confined to the flesh. Their selves are damned by their own constitution. Humanists have argued (against the God of Augustine and Calvin) man's capacity to pull himself up by his own bootstraps. Kafka's souls exemplify the inversion of self-reliance. They have the power to damn themselves.

Dehumanization has become for the twentieth century what *humanitas* was for the Renaissance. The term is now in regular use with reference to modern art, totalitarian democracy, and American advertising. Only human nature is subject to dehumanization, which might best be defined as a studied distortion of what has been held to be distinctively human. While orthodox Christian thinking, and especially Protestantism, always had grave misgivings about any ideal of human self-realization (sin presumably having destroyed man's ability to save himself), the ideal of perfectible humanity has never been altogether absent from the Western tradition. One need only glance at the Madonnas of Renaissance art to sense its powerful appeal. Particularly in the Enlightenment and throughout the nineteenth century humanitarian ideals permeated culture and society. Those who questioned their efficacy became prophets for a future generation. In our day "dehumanization" no longer represents anything startling. Its outlines can be traced through such diverse phenomena as concentration camps, collections of "abstract" paintings, accounts of suburbanite living, and the influence of alumni on higher education. Sometimes, as in Kafka's tales, it manifests itself as an inversion of values, or it may show up as their complete negation, a striking instance of which is the delinquent teen-ager sincerely unaware of having done wrong. Thrill-killing is merely an extreme form of pointless activity. Our present society offers many other more respectable examples, such as the novelty cult.

Most frightening about Kafka's characters (and ourselves) is not their loss of self-identity, but the matter-of-factness with which they accept all that happens to them. If the anarchist and Romantic protest too much, *they* protest too little. This quality of daemonic objectification (quite distinct from Hume's nonchalance) is pointedly conveyed by Kafka's famous opening sentences: "As Gregor Samsa awoke one morning from uneasy dreams he found himself transformed in his bed into a gigantic insect."—"'It is a remarkable piece of apparatus,' said the officer to the explorer and surveyed with a certain air of admiration the apparatus which was after all quite familiar to him."—"During these last decades the interest in professional fasting has markedly diminished."—"I have completed the construction of my burrow and it seems to be successful." To begin with, we are inordinately curious about the life of Gregor Samsa prior to his metamorphosis, and about the life of the officer prior to his assignment to the penal colony; we would like more information on the age or place in which there was interest in professional fasting, and to know exactly what drove the mole to his burrow. These beings appear naturally accommodated to their respective ways of life as if they never knew or wanted any other. Like the stereotype of the German civil service official whose "objectivity" enables him to do the same work for every type of government, Kafka's dehumanized heroes seem oblivious of history and peculiarly lacking in sensitivity. It is testimony to his art that he gets us to suspend our disbelief and to accept their topsy-turvy situations as natural. Kafka has a way of making us feel the absence of passion passionately, of pretending to talk about human subjects as if they were merely clinical objects, and yet forcing us to look through the pretense into the depths beneath.

Many people since Kafka's day have found themselves arrested one fine morning without having had their breakfast. And what is alarming is the growing acceptance of such events as part of being in the world. Bureaucracy must have a debilitating effect on the moral sense. If blowing one's top be associated with adolescence, methodical compliance emerges as a symptom of perversion. The apathetic explorer in the "Penal Colony" is a typical neutral observer, not the amused spectator of the Enlightenment or the passionate Romantic spectator of Kierkegaard's *Diary of the Seducer,* but the selfless self of government agencies. His particular mission is to evaluate the method of execution in use in the penal colony; and it must be admitted that he carries it out admirably. That is to say, he gives offense to no one. Patiently he listens to the officer's case without taking sides. After all, it is not his affair. On the other hand, he refuses to be bribed by the officer into supporting him in front of the New Commandant. Through the turmoil and temptations of the whole unpleasant situation he remains above it all, his own individuality suspended for the sake of external business:

> "There is a prophecy that after a certain number of years the Commandant will rise again and lead his adherents from this house to recover the colony. Have faith and wait!" When the explorer had read this and risen to his feet he saw all the bystanders around him smiling, as if they too had read the inscription, had found it ridiculous and were expecting him to agree with them. The explorer ignored this, distributed a few coins among them, waiting till the table was pushed over the grave again, quitted the teahouse and made for the harbor.[13]

The officer dies voluntarily for his beliefs. It is worth repeating that in his dedication, however diabolical its goal, he comes closer to Kierkegaard's ethical than to the aesthetic stage on life's way. But the explorer remains the embodiment of Jamesian scientism or Kierkegaardian inauthenticity. He is also the most immoral character in the story. The officer, obviously, is possessed and hence beyond the pale of enlightenment; the condemned prisoner has been reduced to helplessness and hence cannot be held accountable for what happens to him; the soldier guarding him is a typical guard. (What can one expect from a broken will under orders?) Of all the individuals implicated in the proceedings the explorer alone is free to speak out with indignation. Perhaps he cannot afford to be righteous. Then again, whatever he does may turn out to be futile; nevertheless, as a fellow human being he is obliged to protest. Here Kant's categorical imperative applies inescapably: "I ought, therefore I can." Yet he does not.

Opportunism is a failing of the uncommitted. This the persecutors and the persecuted are spared. The latter must suffer and the former are condemned to be tormented by guilt and anxiety, but each will preserve at least a remnant of integrity. It is revealing that the characters in Kafka's stories who do not come to a miserable end are the bystanders rather than the participants. Following Gregor's death, his sister on a family outing suggests by her bearing that she is ready for a good match. The explorer, having completed his mission, is off for home and quite conceivably up for a promotion and an honorary degree (doctor of science). The overseer has hit upon a marvelous attraction to replace the hunger artist: the panther. "Even the most insensitive felt it refreshing to see this wild creature leaping around the cage that had so long been dreary." [14] Kafka would have been amused by the new type of successful man in business—the man who reaches the top by virtue of displeasing no one who might prove an obstacle to his advance. To be smoothly self-interested requires above-average intelligence for the concealment of spite. Neither Gregor's sister, nor the overseer, nor the explorer was stupid. An interesting question would be whether Kafka wanted them to know what they were doing.

Conclusion

In her memoirs[1] Simone de Beauvoir describes the restlessness of her generation coming to maturity in the 1920's in these words:

> So immoralism was not just a defiance against society; it was a way of reaching God. Believers and unbelievers alike used this name; according to some, it signified an inaccessible presence, and to others a vertiginous absence: there was no difference, and I had no difficulty in blending Claudel and Gide; in both of them, God was defined, in relationship to the bourgeois world, as the *other,* and everything that was other was a manifestation of something divine. I could recognize the thirst that tortured Nathanael as the emptiness of the heart of Péguy's Joan of Arc and the leprosy gnawing at the flesh of Violaine; there is not much distance between a superhuman sacrifice and a gratuitous crime, and I saw in Synge the sister of Lafcadio. The important thing was to use whatever means one could to find release from the world, and then one could come within reach of eternity.[2]

What she calls the "cult of Restlessness" is the pulse of the Romantic Enlightenment ever moving between two poles: the possibility of the inexistence of God and the possibility of the dehumanization of unbelieving (emancipated) man. All the idealism of the generations from the middle of the eighteenth to the first decades of the twentieth century, whether bourgeois or antibourgeois, was defined by the ambiguities and paradoxes inherent in these options. Bach's music, though firmly anchored in eternity, is not deficient in expressions of uneasiness and dread. Schubert's Wanderer no longer is certain of reaching his destination, but his winter's journey inspires him with melody and thus helps redeem his loneliness and isolation. It is the heroine of Kurt Weill's *Dreigroschenoper,* dreaming of a heavily armed boat that will take her away and annihilate the city, who symbolizes the restlessness of the present—the breakdown of the Romantic Enlightenment.

Pascal's distinction, cited at the beginning of this book, between *esprit de géométrie* and *esprit de finesse* became seminal for the Enlightenment and thereafter. Far more than the other philosophical and theological dualisms going back to antiquity, it continues to govern the spirit of Occidental man. The Romantic Enlightenment brought to a head the conflict between the "reasons of the heart" and that *amor intellectualis* which served Spinoza's sage.

The music of the classical Romantic composers (notably Bach's and Mozart's) embodies a remarkable synthesis of discipline and feeling. Therein the deepest human passions without being glorified, suppressed, or sentimentalized are transformed into instruments of insight and self-knowledge. Bach's and Mozart's perceptual world, for all its orderliness and Apollonian self-possession, remains open to the inroads of the daemonic in human experience. And never is there an absence of feeling, be the work as structured as *The Art of the Fugue* or as gallant as the C-Major Piano Sonata, K.330. What makes their sensibility essentially modern is the controlled interplay between logic (the spirit of geometry) and inwardness (*finesse*). Bach's Passions are free both from the monotony characterizing earlier attempts in the same genre as well as from the blatant bathos of so much nineteenth-century liturgical music. Analogously, Mozart's operas avoid the coldness of Gluck and the frivolity of Rossini, not to mention the bombast of Wagner.

Outside of music this precarious balance was rarely achieved. Pascal's two approaches usually collided, thus leading to one-sided extremes and agonies of double-mindedness. The Romantic Enlightenment arose because traditional forms of feeling and explanation (many of them still rooted in the Middle Ages) proved inadequate to cope with the increasing complexities of modern life. While Hobbes with his implicit faith in civilization viewed nature as an evil condition amenable to proper government, for Rousseau it had already become an idyllic refuge from the ravages of overcivilization. Making due allowance for his exaggerations, Rousseau was right. T. S. Eliot's "hollow men" are not deficient in knowledge and bathroom facilities, but in *esprit de finesse*.

Superficial analyses of the crisis of our age attribute it in large measure to thoughtless action, citing as evidence that time and again even responsible individuals are carried away by prejudice. But is this immaturity basically intellectual? I doubt it. Before Kierkegaard, Pascal and Rousseau, and after him, Nietzsche and Dostoevsky, located the heart of the trouble in a growing process of desensitization. It is a truism worth reiterating that the man with brains can be as narrow and dangerous as the fool. Those who followed Hitler or who speak of winning World War III may indeed be stupid, but their most glaring deficiency lies in the degeneration of what Plato recognized as the spirited part of the soul. The celebrated bankruptcy of the intelligentsia hardly implies a lack of brilliance. One of the principal paradoxes of the twentieth century is the simultaneous manifestation of great scientific achievement and enormous metaphysical failure. The prevalence of meaninglessness in contemporary experience goes hand in hand with the single-minded devotion of "creative" engineers.

Among literary historians in particular it has become commonplace to praise the Augustans (for control) at the expense of the Romantics, who are cut down to size (for excess). Was there ever a more passionate poet than Pope, or one more conscious of form than Keats? Is Flaubert less a Romantic for being emancipated from philistinism, or Dostoevsky less outspoken for associating human salvation with self-sacrifice and inner freedom? At its best, the Romantic Enlightenment exemplified a rare alliance of forthright statement and strong involvement. Had the "Grand Inquisitor" episode from *The Brothers Karamazov* been written in the seventeenth century, surely reprisals would have been taken against its author. The *philosophes* could never have conceived such a scene, not because they lacked the necessary freedom and daring, but because their hatred of the clergy blinded them to such alternatives to Christendom as anticlerical theism. They had a compulsion to throw out the baby with the bath. Nevertheless, Voltaire's mockery felicitously fused with Romantic longing is what makes Ivan's account of the Second Coming an unforgettable piece of religious testimony. Ivan and Alyosha in arguing the ultimate questions are completely emancipated. Yet in stark contrast to Hume and Gibbon their attitude is anything but smug or nonchalant. They also entertain the notion of God's inexistence. On the other hand, no longer do they draw the naïve inference that this must spell unwonted happiness for man.

In writing this book I set out to trace the gradual breakdown of the precarious but creatively fruitful union of *esprit de géométrie* and *esprit de finesse*. Broadly speaking, some pattern like the following emerges: The spirit of geometry became distorted into scientism in religion, cubism in art, ideology in politics, and positivism in metaphysics. Meanwhile, *finesse* degenerated correspondingly into innocuous piety, impressionistic fragments or expressionistic raptures, crass utilitarianism, and the deification of the point of view. Kantian critical understanding degenerated either into hairsplitting, or through Fichte and Hegel, once again became pretentious and dogmatic reason. Analogously, the remarkable sensitivity of Rousseau (starting with Rousseau himself) led to the worst kind of arrogance and sentimentality. Wagner's *Parsifal* is to *The Magic Flute* what Nietzsche's *Thus Spake Zarathustra* represents vis-à-vis Schopenhauer's *The World as Will and Idea*.

Not only did subjectivity and reflection proceed separately, but like Marx in relation to Hegel, soon each was turned upside down. If the genius of Tchaikovsky was limited by a disregard for measure, the greatness of Richard Strauss's music is often marred by his need to parody, satirize, and evoke the nostalgic mood. Here it is not a question of untransfigured overwroughtness but rather of a fear of being oneself.

Running parallel to the inversion of subjectivity is that of reflection. Critics of Kierkegaard, Dostoevsky, and Nietzsche persist in confusing their attack on the idolatry of intelligence with irrationalism or anti-intellectualism. It is hard to think of three men more intellectually oriented than these. Especially illuminating in this regard are the novels of Dostoevsky in which the great sinners do not suffer for using their minds, but for using them against themselves and society. Inspector Porfiry in *Crime and Punishment* is more than a match in critical intelligence to Raskolnikov. But the police inspector, notwithstanding his brilliance and position in society, remains humane and kind while Raskolnikov, the destitute young idealist bent on reforming the world, does not.

Until modern times wickedness was generally conceded to spring from the passions getting the better of reason. This Greek way of thinking about human emotion, whatever its pedagogical justification in the past, proved inadequate. The real danger in modern times comes from those who think ruthlessly like Gide's Immoralist and Thomas Mann's Adrian Leverkühn. Corresponding to the prostitution of subjectivity into sentimentality is the betrayal of the intellect by illusions of potential omniscience. Pascal, with his unique acumen, had foreseen these possibilities in stressing (over against Descartes) the frailty of man, whom he likened to a "thinking reed."

The Romantic Enlightenment passed through three distinct phases. In the first (roughly speaking from Bach's death in 1750 to the death of Hegel in 1831), there was general rejoicing over the ambiguities of an emancipated intelligence in rapport with spontaneous emotion. This state of affairs can be symbolized in musical terms by the development of fugue and sonata form. In the second phase (lasting roughly to the onset of Nietzsche's insanity, in 1888) emotion and intelligence drew further and further apart, each excelling by itself but beginning to miss the support of its partner. Musically this corresponds to the *Lied* and the emergence of virtuoso performers. In the third period (ending about the time of Kafka's death, in 1924) there occurs an overreaching both of emotion and reflection. Strangeness and distortion are pursued for their own sake. Jazz and twelve-tone music constitute a fundamental break with more than three centuries of Occidental music—the one reaching an almost universal audience, the other an esoteric elite.

This so far has been the story of the Romantic Enlightenment. Surely its breakdown should not obscure its triumphs.

Selected Bibliography

Sources used in the body of the book are indicated in the Notes. The writings of Kant, Dostoevsky, Kierkegaard, Hume, and William James are readily available in numerous editions. The books listed below have been more or less central to my purpose in the preparation of the present work.

BOOKS ABOUT THE ROMANTIC ENLIGHTENMENT:

Barth, Karl. *Die protestantische Theologie im 19. Jahrhundert*, 1947. Published in English as *Protestant Thought: From Rousseau to Ritschl*. New York, 1959.

Baeck, Leo. *Judaism and Christianity* (tr. W. Kaufmann). New York, 1958.

Becker, C. L. *The Heavenly City of the Eighteenth Century Philosophers*. New Haven, 1932.

Benjamin, Walter. *Schriften*. Frankfurt am Main, 1955.

Carr, E. H. *The Romantic Exiles*. New York, 1933.

Cassirer, Ernst. *The Philosophy of the Enlightenment*. Princeton, 1951.

Dilthey, Wilhelm. *Leben Schleiermachers*. Berlin, 1870.

———. *Friedrich der Grosse und die Deutsche Aufklärung*. Berlin, 1927.

———. *Die Jugendgeschichte Hegels*. Stuttgart, 1959.

Dodwell, Henry. *Christianity Not Founded on Argument, And the True Principle of Gospel-Evidence Assigned: In a Letter to a Young Gentleman at Oxford*. London, 1741.

Frank, Erich. *Philosophical Understanding and Religious Truth*. New York, 1945.

Gross, Helmut. *Der deutsche Idealismus und das Christen-*

tum: Versuch einer vergleichenden Phenomonologie. Munich, 1927.

Guardini, Romano. *Gegensatz.* Mainz, 1925.

Gundolph, Friedrich. *Romantiker.* Berlin, 1936.

Hamburger, Michael. *Reason and Energy: Studies in German Literature.* New York, 1957.

Hazard, Paul. *The European Mind 1680-1715.* London, 1953.

————. *European Thought in the 18th Century.* London, 1954.

Heer, Friedrich. *Europäische Geistesgeschichte.* Stuttgart, 1953.

Heiss, Robert. *Der Gang des Geistes: Eine Geschichte des neuzeitlichen Denkens.* Bern, 1948.

Heller, Erich. *The Disinherited Mind.* London, 1952.

Herold, J. Christopher. *Mistress to an Age: A Life of Madame de Staël.* New York, 1958.

Hirsch, Emanuel. *Geschichte der neuen evangelischen Theologie im Zusammenhang mit den allgemeinen Bewegungen des europäischen Denkens.* Volumes 1-5. Gütersloh, 1949-54.

Hoffmann, E. T. A. *Betrachtungen über Musik.* Stuttgart, 1947.

Husserl, Edmund. *Die Krisis der europäischen Wissenschaften und die transzendental Phaenomenologie.* The Hague, 1954.

Kahler, Erich. *The Tower and the Abyss.* New York, 1957.

Kayser, Wolfgang. *Das Groteske: Seine Gestaltung in Malerei und Dichtung.* Hamburg, 1957.

Kendrick, T. D. *The Lisbon Earthquake.* London, 1956.

Kroner, Richard. *Von Kant bis Hegel.* Tübingen, 1921-4.

Krueger, Gerhard. *Grundfragen der Philosophie, Geschichte, Wahrheit, Wissenschaft.* Frankfurt am Main, 1958.

Löwith, Karl. *Kierkegaard und Nietzsche oder die theologische und philosophische Überwindung des Nihilismus.* Frankfurt am Main, 1933.

————. *Von Hegel zu Nietzsche: Der revolutionäre Bruch im Denken des neunzehnten Jahrhundert.* Zurich, 1941.

Luetgert, Wilhelm. *Die Religion des deutschen Idealismus und ihr Ende.* Gütersloh, 1923.

Lukács, G. *Die Zerstörung der Vernunft.* Berlin, 1954.

Mannheim, Karl. *Ideology and Utopia.* London, 1936.

Manuel, Frank E. *The Eighteenth Century Confronts the Gods.* Cambridge, 1959.

Marcuse, Herbert. *Reason and Revolution.* New York-London, 1941.

Ortega y Gasset, José. *Man and Crisis.* New York, 1958.

———. *Man and People.* New York, 1957.

———. *The Revolt of the Masses.* New York, 1932.

Rehm, Walter. *Experimentum Medietatis: Studien zur Geistes und Literaturgeschichte des 19. Jahrhundert.* Munich, 1947.

Schiller, Friedrich. *On the Aesthetic Education of Man* (tr. R. Snell). New Haven, 1954.

Schlatter, Adolph. *Die philosophische Arbeit seit Cartesius, nach ihrem ethischen und religiösen Ertrag.* Gütersloh, 1906.

Schnabel, Franz. *Deutsche Geschichte im neunzehnten Jahrhundert.* Volumes 1 and 4. Freiburg, 1948 and 1951.

Schmitt, Carl. *Politische Romantik.* Munich and Leipzig, 1925.

Schneider, Reinhold. *Die Heimkehr des deutschen Geistes: Das Bild Christi in der deutschen Philosophie des 19. Jahrhunderts.* Heidelberg, 1946.

Sedlmayr, Hans. *Verlust der Mitte: Die Bildende Kunst des 19. und 20. Jahrhunderts als Symptom und Symbol der Zeit.* Salzburg, 1948. Translated by Brian Battershaw under title of *Art in Crisis: the Lost Center.* Chicago, 1958.

Thévénaz, Pierre. *L'Homme et sa raison.* Neuchâtel, 1956.

Tillich, Paul. *Das Dämonische: Ein Beitrag zur Sinndeutung der Geschichte.* Tübingen, 1926.

———. *The Interpretation of History.* New York, 1936.

Troeltsch, Ernst. *Der Historismus und seine Probleme.* Tübingen, 1922.

Wandruszka, Mario. *Der Geist der französischen Sprache.* Hamburg, 1959.

Willey, Basil. *The 17th Century Background*. London, 1934.

————. *The 18th Century Background*. London, 1941.

————. *Nineteenth Century Studies*. London, 1949.

————. *More Nineteenth Century Studies*. London, 1956.

Williams, Raymond. *Culture and Society*. New York, 1958.

BOOKS ABOUT KIERKEGAARD:

Collins, James. *The Mind of Kierkegaard*. Chicago, 1953.

Diem, Hermann. *Kierkegaard: Dialectic of Existence* (tr. Harold Wright). London, 1959.

Hoeffding, H. *Sören Kierkegaard*. Stuttgart, 1896.

Swenson, David F. *Something about Kierkegaard*. Minneapolis, 1945.

Thomas, J. Heywood. *Subjectivity and Paradox: A Study of Kierkegaard*. New York, 1957.

Thust, Martin. *Sören Kierkegaard: der Dichter des religiösen Grundlagen eines Systems der Subjektivität*. Munich, 1931.

Wyschogrod, Michael. *Kierkegaard and Heidegger: The Ontology of Existence*. London, 1954.

BOOKS ABOUT MOZART:

Dent, Edward Joseph. *Mozart's Operas: A Critical Study*. London, 1913.

Einstein, Alfred. *Mozart: His Character, His Work*. Oxford, 1945.

Gounod, Charles François. *Le Don Juan de Mozart*. Paris, 1890.

Hocquard, Jean-Victor. *La Pensée de Mozart*. Paris, 1958.

Jahn, Otto. *W. A. Mozart*. Edited by Hermann Abert. Leipzig, 1923-4.

Pieger, Karl (ed.). *Urteile bedeutender Dichter, Philosophen und Musiker über Mozart*. Wiesbaden, 1886.

Turner, Walter James. *Mozart: The Man and His Works*. New York, 1938.

Valentin, Erich. *Wege zu Mozart mit Briefen, Urteilen der Zeitgenossen und der Nachwelt*. Regensburg, 1941.

BOOKS ABOUT HUME:

Basson, A. H. *David Hume*. Harmondsworth, 1958.

Hendel, C. W., Jr. *Studies in the Philosophy of David Hume*. Princeton, 1925.

Mossner, E. C. *Life of David Hume*. Austin, Texas, 1954.

Smith, Norman Kemp. *Philosophy of David Hume*. London, 1941.

BOOKS ABOUT WILLIAM JAMES:

Matthiessen, F. O. *The James Family*. New York, 1947.

Perry, R. B. *The Thought and Character of William James*. Boston, 1935.

BOOKS ABOUT DOSTOEVSKY:

Berdyaev, Nicholas. *Dostoyevsky: An Interpretation*. New York, 1934.

Gide, André. *Dostoyevsky*. Paris, 1923.

Guardini, Romano. *Der Mensch und der Glaube: Versuche über die religiöse Existenz in Dostoyevskys grossen Romanen*. Leipzig, 1933.

Jackson, Robert L. *Dostoevsky's Underground Man in Russian Literature*. The Hague, 1958.

Steiner, George. *Tolstoy or Dostoevsky*. New York, 1959.

Zweig, Stefan. *Die Baumeister der Welt*. Vol. 1. Leipzig, 1929.

BOOKS ABOUT KAFKA:

Anders, Günther. *Kafka Pro & Contra*. Munich, 1951.

Gray, Ronald D. *Kafka's Castle*. Cambridge, 1956.

Wagenbach, Klaus. *Franz Kafka: Eine Biographie seiner Jugend*. Bern, 1958.

Weltsch, Felix. *Religion und Humor im Leben und Werk Franz Kafkas*. Berlin, 1957.

Notes

Introduction

[1] *The Autobiography of Mark Rutherford* [William Hale White] (London, 1881), p. 80.

[2] Ibid., p. 85.

[3] Ibid., pp. 89-90.

[4] Geoffrey Scott, *The Portrait of Zélide* (New York, 1959), pp. 133-5.

I. The Breakdown of Universal Order

[1] "The Real Greatness of Mozart in Modern Eyes" (*Nouvelle Revue Française* [Nov. 1937]), tr. Angelo P. Bertocci in *From the N.R.F.*, edited with an introduction by Justin O'Brien (New York, 1958), p. 218.

[2] Karl Barth, *"Die kirchliche Dogmatik,"* III, 3 (Zurich, 1950), pp. 337-9.

[3] (Zurich, 1956), tr. Walter M. Mosse, in *Religion and Culture: Essays in Honor of Paul Tillich*, ed. W. Leibrecht (New York, 1959), pp. 61-78. Professor James Luther Adams called my attention to yet another treatment of Mozart in Barth's writings. In his history of nineteenth-century Protestant theology Barth singles out Mozart and Kant as the two "giants" of the Enlightenment who acknowledged limits to human sovereignty. The statue of the Commendatore in *Don Giovanni* vainly calling the Don to repentance represents the irrepressible claims of conscience.

[4] Cf. *Either/Or: A Fragment of Life*, tr. David F. and Lillian M. Swenson, I (Princeton, 1949), pp. 35-111.

[5] Lenau's Don Juan, for example, kills himself out of ennui when on the verge of final success. In *Don Giovanni* he does appear a failure in his amatory exploits, yet it would contradict his essential nature to despair of tangible accomplishments, for then he would have ceased to be authentically daemonic or single-mindedly dedicated to the quest and realization of one aim only. Girls had good cause to be afraid

of him, but not of his "Hamlet-like" successors as the romantic poets drew them.

[6] Cf. *The Sickness unto Death*, tr., with an introduction by
Walter Lowrie (Princeton, 1946), pp. 46 ff. See Chapter IV
below.

[7] Within Mozart's musical framework the ending of *Don
Giovanni* is not as atypical as often supposed. Many instrumental and chamber works follow the same pattern of tremendous tension being built up in the earlier movements to
be succeeded by an unexpected "light" or exuberant finale.
For examples, I would call special attention to the piano concertos K.466 and K.595; the G-minor Quintet, K.516; the
Sinfonia Concertante, K.364; the B-flat Divertimento, K.287;
the "Posthorn" Serenade, K.320; and the C-major Symphony,
K.338. To be sure, in works such as the "Jupiter" Symphony
and the D-major Quintet, K.593, there is a process of consummation with the "appropriate" climax. The point is that
some of Mozart's best compositions from all periods do not
follow this form, and that deviation far from being a letdown
may serve as a unique enhancement. Truly remarkable is the
change of mood in the "Posthorn" Serenade. This is intended
to be festive music. But the fifth movement, the Andantino,
explores the depths of human suffering. It seems utterly incongruous. Then follows a minuet that in turn gives way to
a furious finale with a remarkable development section. Like
human destiny the flow of Mozart's inspiration is unpredictable.

[8] Cf. Chapter IV.

[9] Cf. Chapter V.

[10] Man, wandering on his road must bear the tribulation
    Of fire and water, earth and air's probation.
    If he prevails against the lures of evil's might,
    He soon will know the joys of heaven's light.
    Enlightened, he will now himself prepare,
    The holy mysteries of Isis all to share.

The English version is by Ruth and Thomas Martin (New
York, 1941).

[11] *Fear and Trembling* in *Fear and Trembling and The
Sickness unto Death*, tr. with introduction and notes by Walter
Lowrie (New York, 1955), pp. 58-9.

[12] In fairness to Kierkegaard it must be emphasized that his
category of the purely aesthetic was intended as a typological
abstraction that as much may exist only in infants or irre-

sponsibles. But if most forms of the aesthetic mode of existence are reflective as well as sensual, how can music fail to have ethical-religious content, being so closely tied to the inner life of man?

[13] This essentially was the view of Goethe, Stendhal, Rossini, and Schumann.

[14] For a general discussion of this category cf. Introduction, pp. 24 ff.

II. The Breakdown of Criticism

[1] *The Portrait of Zélide* (New York, 1959), p. 164.

[2] *David Hume* (Harmondsworth, 1958), p. 150.

[3] *A Group of Honest Doubters* (London, 1956).

[4] David Hume, *Dialogues Concerning Natural Religion,* edited with an introduction by Henry D. Aiken. (New York, 1951), p. 7.

[5] Cf. Chapter III.

[6] *Dialogues,* pp. 31-2.

[7] Cf. Chapter V.

[8] *Dialogues,* p. 32.

[9] Cf. Chapter III.

[10] *Training in Christianity,* p. 98.

[11] *Dialogues,* pp. 13-14.

[12] Ibid., p. 67.

[13] Ibid., pp. 61, 63.

[14] Here again Hume proves a perspicacious critic of his time: "Formerly [Philo speaking], it was a most popular theological topic to maintain that human life was vanity and misery, and to exaggerate all the ills and pains which are incident to men. But of late years, divines, we find, begin to retract this position and maintain, though still with some hesitation, that there are more goods than evils, more pleasures than pains, even in this life." Ibid., p. 80.

[15] Ibid., pp. 41, 79.

[16] Cf. Chapter IV.

[17] "There is no view of human life or the condition of mankind from which, without the greatest violence, we can infer the moral attributes or learn that infinite benevolence, conjoined with infinite power and infinite wisdom, which we must discover by the eyes of faith alone." *Dialogues,* p. 70.

"Is the world considered in general and as it appears to us in this life, different from what a man or such a limited being would, *beforehand,* expect from a very powerful, wise, and benevolent Deity? It must be strange prejudice to assert the contrary. . . ." Ibid., p. 73.

"A person seasoned with a just sense of the imperfections of natural reason, will fly to revealed truth with the greatest avidity, while the haughty dogmatist, persuaded that he can erect a complete system of theology by the mere help of philosophy, disdains any further aid and rejects this adventitious instructor. To be a philosophical sceptic is, in a man of letters, the first and most essential step towards being a sound, believing Christian. . . ." Ibid., p. 80.

III. *The Breakdown of Empirical Certainty*

[1] *Prolegomena to Any Future Metaphysics* (New York, 1950), p. 106.

[2] Since this chapter was written, James has been treated in this way by H. Stuart Hughes in *Consciousness and Society: The Reorientation of European Social Thought, 1890-1930* (New York, 1958). Cf. also Julius Seelye Bixler, "The Existentialists and William James," *The American Scholar* (Winter, 1958-9), pp. 80-90.

[3] This was called to my attention by Professor Mary Mothersill.

[4] *The Letters of William James,* selected and edited with biographical introduction and notes by his son Henry James (Boston, 1920), Vol. II, pp. 131-2.

[5] Ibid., Vol. I, pp. 309-11.

[6] Ibid., Vol. I, pp. 145-7; also *The Varieties of Religious Experience* (New York, 1929), pp. 157-8.

[7] Ibid., Vol. I, pp. 263-4.

[8] "I ought to give a message with a practical outcome and an emotional musical accompaniment, so to speak, fitted to interest men as men, and yet also not altogether to disappoint philosophers—since philosophers, let them be as queer as they will, still are men in the secret recesses of their hearts, even here at Berkeley."—"Philosophical Conceptions and Practical Results," *Collected Essays and Reviews* (New York, 1920), pp. 406-7.

"The whole function of philosophy ought to be to find out what definite differences it will make to you and me, at definite instants of our life, if this world formula or that world formula be the one which is true."—Ibid., pp. 413-14.

"What accounts do the nethermost bounds of the universe

owe to me? By what insatiate conceit and lust of intellectual despotism do I arrogate the right to know their secrets, and from my philosophic throne to play the only airs I shall march to, as if I were the Lord's anointed?"—"On Some Hegelisms," *The Will to Believe and Other Essays in Popular Philosophy* (New York, 1917), p. 277.

"Philosophies, whether expressed in sonnets or systems, must all wear this form. The thinker starts from some experience of the practical world, and asks its meaning. He launches himself upon the speculative sea, and makes a voyage long or short. He ascends into the empyrean, and communes with the eternal essences. But whatever his achievements and discoveries be while gone, the utmost result they can issue in is some new practical maxim or resolve, or the denial of some old one, with which inevitably he is sooner or later washed ashore on the *terra firma* of concrete life again."—"Reflex Action and Theism," *The Will to Believe and Other Essays in Popular Philosophy* (New York, 1917), pp. 142-3.

[9] "The true objection to materialism is not positive but negative. . . . We make complaint of it for what it is *not*—not a permanent warrant for our more ideal interests, not a fulfiller of our remotest hopes."—"Philosophical Conceptions and Practical Results," *Collected Essays and Reviews*, p. 422.

"If we are to choose which is the more essential factor of human character, the fighting virtue or the intellectual breadth, we must side with Tolstoi, and choose that simple faithfulness to his light or darkness which any common unintellectual man can show."—"What Makes a Life Significant," *On Some of Life's Ideals* (New York, 1913), p. 86.

"If a thinker had no stake in the unknown, no vital needs, to live or languish according to what the unseen world contained, a philosophic neutrality and refusal to believe either one way or the other would be his wisest cue. But, unfortunately, neutrality is not only inwardly difficult, it is also outwardly unrealizable, where our relations to an alternative are both practical and vital."—*Is Life Worth Living* (Philadelphia, 1896), p. 23.

"The preferences of sentient creatures are what *create* the importance of topics. . . . And I for my part cannot but consider the talk of the contemporary sociological school about averages and general laws and predetermined tendencies, with its obligatory undervaluing of the importance of individual differences, as the most pernicious and immoral of fatalisms. Suppose there is a social equilibrium fated to be, whose is it to be,—that of your preference, or mine? There lies the question of questions, and it is one which no study of averages can decide."—"The Importance of Individuals," *The Will to Believe and Other Essays,* p. 256.

"But into every fact in which there enters an element of personal contribution on my part, as soon as this personal contribution demands a certain degree of subjective energy which, in its turn, calls for a certain amount of faith in its result— so that, after all, the future fact is conditioned by my present faith in it—how trebly asinine would it be for me to deny myself *the use of the subjective method,* the method of belief based on desire. . . . If M represents the entire world minus the reaction of the thinker upon it, and if M plus x represent the absolutely total matter of philosophic propositions (x standing for the thinker's reactions and its results)—what would be a universal truth if the term x were of one complexion, might become egregious error if x altered its character. Let it not be said that x is too infinitesimal a component to change the character of the immense whole in which it lies imbedded. Everything depends on the point of view of the philosophic proposition in question."—"The Sentiment of Rationality," *Essays in Pragmatism* (New York, 1948), pp. 27-8.

[10] Kierkegaard's analysis of anxiety in *The Sickness unto Death* and Heidegger's of *Sorge* in *Sein und Zeit* are outstanding achievements in these directions.

[11] "Truly enough, the details vanish in the bird's eye view; so does the bird's eye view vanish in the details. Which is the right point of view for philosophic vision? Nature gives no reply, for both points of view being equally real, are equally natural; and no one natural reality *per se* is any more emphatic than any other. Accentuation, foreground, and background are created solely by the interested attention of the looker on. . . ." —"The Importance of Individuals," *The Will to Believe and Other Essays,* p. 256.

"If there be such (universal or divine) consciousness, then its demands carry the most of obligation simply because they are the greatest in amount. But it is even then not *abstractly* right that we should respect them. It is only *concretely* right —or right after the fact, or by virtue of the fact, that they are actually made. Suppose that we do not respect them, as seems largely to be the case in this queer world. That ought not to be, we say; that is wrong. But in what way is the fact of wrongness made more acceptable or intelligible when we imagine it to consist rather in the laceration of an *apriori* ideal order than in the disappointment of a living personal God? Do we perhaps think that we cover God and protect him and make his importance over us less ultimate, when we back him up with this *apriori* blanket from which he may draw some warmth of further appeal?"—"The Moral Philosopher and the Moral Life," *Essays in Pragmatism*, pp. 73-4.

"Every Jack sees in his own particular Jill charms and perfections to the enchantment of which we stolid onlookers are stone-cold. And which has the superior view of the absolute truth, he or we? Which has the more vital insight into the nature of Jill's existence, as a fact? Is he in excess, being in this matter a maniac? or are we in defect, being victims of a pathological anaesthesia as regards Jill's magical importance? Surely the latter; surely to Jack are the profounder truths revealed. For Jack realizes Jill concretely, and we do not. He struggles towards a union with her inner life, divining her feelings, anticipating her desires, understanding her limits as manfully as he can, and yet inadequately, too; for he is also inflicted with some blindness, even here. Whilst we, dead clods that we are, do not even seek after these things, but are contented that the portion of eternal fact named Jill should be for us as if it were not. Jill, who knows her inner life, knows that Jack's way of taking it—so importantly—is the true and serious way; and she responds to the truths in him by taking him truly and seriously, too. May the ancient blindness never wrap its clouds about either of them again! Where would any of *us* be, were there no one willing to know us as we really are or to repay us for *our* insight by making recognizant return? We ought, all of us, to realize each other in this intense, pathetic, and important way." —"What Makes a Life Significant," *On Some of Life's Ideals*, pp. 50-1.

[12] Its history dates back to Socrates, although the term was first popularized by Leslie Stephen. Socrates did not know what would happen to his soul after death, but his faith in virtue as knowledge and goodness as its own reward was unaffected by immortality—one way or the other. The deists in the eighteenth century were basically agnostic. Most important to them was the advancement of science and the diffusion of cosmopolitanism among some of the less enlightened. Their religious tolerance was to a large extent the concomitance of indifference. Hume, as I tried to show in Chapter II, recognized this very clearly in satirizing the dubious theism of his

educated contemporaries through Philo. Indeed the Enlightenment by and large did not risk taking much of a stand on the religious issue.

[13] "To eat our cake and have it, to love our soul and save it, to enjoy the physical privilege of selfishness and the moral luxury of altruism at the same time, would be ideal. *But the real offers us these tensions in the shape of mutually exclusive alternatives of which only one can be true at once; so that we must choose, and in choosing murder one possibility. The wrench is absolute: 'Either-or!'* . . . Just as whenever I bet a hundred dollars on an event, there comes an instant when I am a hundred dollars richer or poorer without any intermediate degrees passed over; just as my wavering between a journey to Portland or New York does not carry me from Cambridge in a resultant direction in which both motions are compounded, say to Albany, but at a given moment results in the conjunction of reality in all its fullness for one alternative and impossibility in all its fullness for the other—so the bachelor joys are utterly lost from the law of being for the married man, who must henceforth find his in something that is not them but is good enough to make him forget them; so the careless and irresponsible living, the unbuttoning after supper and sleeping upon beaches in the afternoon, are stars that have set upon the path of him who in good earnest makes himself a moralist. *The transitions are abrupt, absolute, truly shot out of a pistol; for while many possibilities are called, the few that are chosen are chosen in all their sudden completeness.*"—"On Some Hegelisms," *The Will to Believe and Other Essays in Popular Philosophy*, p. 269 (Italics mine. G. C.).

"*Why, doubt itself is a decision of the widest practical reach, if only because we may miss by doubting what goods we might be gaining by espousing the winning side. But more than that! It is often practically impossible to distinguish doubt from dogmatic negation.* If I refuse to stop a murder because I am in doubt whether it be not justifiable homicide, I am virtually abetting crime. If I refuse to bale out a boat because I am in doubt whether my efforts will help keep her afloat, I am really helping to sink her. *If in the mountain precipice I doubt my right to risk a leap, I actively connive at my destruction.* He who commands himself not to be credulous of God, of duty, of freedom, of immortality, may again and again be indistinguishable from him who dogmatically denies them. *Scepticism in moral matters is an active ally of immorality. Who is not for is against. The universe will have no neutrals in these questions. In theory as in practice, dodge or hedge, or talk as we like about a wise scepticism, we are really doing volunteer military service for one side or the other.*"—"The Sentiment of Rationality," *Essays in Pragmatism,* pp. 35-6 (Italics mine. G. C.).

[14] Book Six, Chapters IV and V, translated and edited by Albert C. Cutler, Volume VII, *The Library of Christian Classics* (Philadelphia, 1955) (Italics mine. G. C.).

[15] A further important instance of James's overoptimism occurs in his essay "The Moral Equivalent of War." After finding both pacifism and militant nationalism wanting as ideals in the modern world, the one because of its bestial and suicidal aspects and the other because it does not do justice to the virtues of military life and invites degeneration, he makes his celebrated proposal that young men be conscripted to a life of duty where instead of killing each other they would be required to submit to adventure, danger, and self-discipline in raising the level of backward areas everywhere. Thus the positive aspects of a dedicated existence would be conjoined with humanitarianism rather than destruction. So far so good, in theory. But James cannot resist ending his delightful little essay with the following reflections, extremely bittersweet in the light of our later twentieth-century experience:

"Wells adds that he thinks that the conceptions of order and discipline, the tradition of service and devotion, of physical fitness, unstinted exertion, and universal responsibility, which universal military duty is now teaching European nations, will remain a permanent acquisition, when the last ammunition has been used in the fireworks that celebrate the final peace. I believe as he does. It would be simply preposterous if the only force that could work ideals of honor and standards of efficiency into English or American natures should be the fear of being killed by the Germans or the Japanese. Great indeed is Fear; but it is not, as our military enthusiasts believe and try to make us believe, the only stimulus known for awakening the higher ranges of men's spiritual energy. The amount of alteration in public opinion which my utopia postulates is vastly less than the difference between the mentality of those black warriors who pursued Stanley's party on the Congo with their cannibal war-cry of 'Meat! Meat!' and that of the 'general staff' of any civilized nation. History has seen the latter interval bridged over: the former one can be bridged over much more easily."—"The Moral Equivalent of War," published by the American Association for International Conciliation, February, 1910, No. 27, 20.

One wonders, e.g., how James would have accounted for the behavior of the German general staff so long as Hitler appeared to be winning the Second World War.

[16] "The Will to Believe," *Essays in Pragmatism*, p. 106.

[17] "The Sentiment of Rationality," *Essays in Pragmatism*, p. 27.

[18] "The Will to Believe," *Essays in Pragmatism*, pp. 104-5.

[19] *The Varieties of Religious Experience*, p. 23.

[20] Ibid., p. 160.

[21] Ibid., p. 356.

[22] To what extent, if any, James made personal use of "the will to believe" cannot be determined. Certain it is that he was neither an orthodox Christian nor, like Dewey, a satisfied humanist. Perhaps his position is best described as heretical Christian realism anticipating Niebuhrian neo-orthodoxy.

[23] *The Varieties of Religious Experience*, pp. 426-7.

[24] Cf. pp. 480, 481, 488.

[25] Ibid., pp. 481-2.

IV. The Breakdown of Autonomy

[1] *The Sickness unto Death* in *Fear and Trembling and The Sickness unto Death*, tr. with introduction and notes by Walter Lowrie (New York, 1955), p. 150.

[2] Fyodor Dostoevsky, *Letters from the Underworld*, translated with an introduction by C. J. Hogarth (London, 1913. Last reprinted 1953).

[3] *The Sickness unto Death*, p. 206.

[4] Like Pascal, Kierkegaard, even after his conversion, was profoundly influenced by secular thought. Dostoevsky came closer to being a "spiritualist" than a "churched" Christian writer.

[5] Cf. Chapter V.

[6] This was William James's main theme in "The Will to Believe." Cf. the previous chapter.

[7] Dostoevsky, *Letters from the Underworld*, pp. 25-7.

[8] Ibid., pp. 28-9.

[9] Ibid., pp. 33-4.

[10] Ibid., p. 45.

[11] Cf. Kierkegaard, *The Sickness unto Death*, pp. 245 ff.

[12] Cf. ibid., pp. 152 ff. A remarkable anticipation of Kafka's story "Metamorphosis."

[13] *Letters from the Underworld*, p. 47.

14 All the headings to be used are taken from *The Sickness unto Death*. Below each heading I shall cite parallel passages from it and *Letters from the Underworld* prior to following through on the analysis of the point up for discussion. The order in which the nature and forms of despair are considered here is also roughly Kierkegaard's own.

15 Cf. below.

16 Cf. pp. 127-8.

17 See Chapter VII.

18 *The Sickness unto Death*, pp. 157-8.

19 The Underground Man stubbornly clings to his despair as if thereby he could assuage his disgust with the outside world and with himself. Instead of using his powers of observation and great sensitivity as means to arriving at a truer mode of existence, he tries to consume himself in anger and bitterness. From the ethical point of view, certainly, his lingering in despair makes him progressively more unkind and malicious. There is an analogy between the potential for good and evil of a despairer and the responses of individuals to disaster. No doubt, as a general truth, the riot squads must be kept in readiness to prevent rape, looting, etc. But just as probable is the hypothesis that some individuals will find themselves in the course of such a crisis. For them, if not vicariously for the rest of society, the disaster turned out a blessing in disguise. From the Christian point of view, despair is the sickness unto death for which faith is the only cure, but it may also be the cure of self-complacency and self-righteousness. This, I take it, is what Kierkegaard means by its dialectical nature.

20 *The Sickness unto Death*, pp. 166, 169.

21 Ibid., pp. 163 ff.

22 In *Stages on Life's Way* Kierkegaard speaks of "dethronement," which likewise means that no stage is ever entirely canceled out.

23 *The Sickness unto Death*, pp. 149-50.

24 "If I seem to speak exultantly it's only because my intellect enjoys the clear perception of a fact," remarks Jasper Milains, the immoralist in Gissing's *New Grubb Street*.

25 This limitation in Greek thought emerges with particular sharpness in Plato's conception of the ruling class in his *Republic*. How could he possibly assume that any group of men, select as they might be, could be trusted to act selflessly over a long period of time? To be sure, Plato entertained grave doubts about finding candidates for the job of philosopher-king. But this is only a preliminary problem. The real

issue, for a Christian, consists in the sinfulness of all men however intelligent, well-trained, and detached they might be. Lord Acton's famous dictum on power is the prolegomena to any Christian political philosophy. No form of government is a priori beyond suspicion, which is not to argue that one may not be superior to the rest. It is a question of deciding for the least potentially sinful kind. And here much, though by no means every consideration, favors democracy, where checks and balances are imposed on the sinfulness of men in power. Had Kierkegaard and Dostoevsky been understood when the twentieth century began, some of the outrages perpetrated by civilized society might, if not prevented, at least have come as less of a shock.

[26] Cf. pp. 109-10 above.

[27] *Letters from the Underworld,* pp. 140-1.

[28] *The Sickness unto Death,* p. 200. A remarkable instance of such behavior is provided by Cicero in his *Tusculan Disputations,* Book V, Chapter 20 (¶57): therein Cicero describes how the tyrant Dionysios, having jokingly suggested to a friend that the latter had the opportunity to kill him, ordered the friend to be slain when he laughed at the joke. I am grateful to Mr. Paul Eisenberg for calling my attention to this classical episode.

[29] According to Kierkegaard, it is for precisely this reason that God had to become flesh. Only the lowliest of men—most-powerful incognito—could effectively identify with publicans and sinners.

[30] *The Sickness unto Death,* p. 217.

[31] *Letters from the Underworld,* p. 20.

V. *The Breakdown of Faith*

[1] *Letters from the Underworld,* p. 21.

[2] Cf. below.

[3] Cf. Chapter II.

[4] Thomas Mann, *Death in Venice and Seven Other Stories* (New York, 1954), p. 140.

[5] *Journey to Java.*

[6] Obviously this does not apply to the classical left-wing intellectual whose ideological commitments invariably fail to jibe with the critical spirit that led him to their espousal. Aside from this, a serious difficulty must be admitted here. Ours is not an age of faith—James is quite correct in his diagnosis—yet at the same time it is an age that has elicited blind obedience from millions. But, as must be clear from the

foregoing, the meaning of faith here is a different one from that which a demagogue would attach to the loyalty of his supporters. A man of faith in the genuine sense stands up for what he believes and does not allow himself to be hypnotized into mass submission. Marxists, significantly enough, do not bear witness to what the truth means for them, but submit to the anonymous orders of a Party.

VI. The Breakdown of Virtue

[1] Page 45.

[2] Cf. Kant, *Gesammelte Schriften* (Berlin, 1902-41), VII, 63.

[3] Cf. *"Über ein Vermeintes Recht aus Menschenliebe zu Lügen,"* ibid., VIII, 427 ff.

[4] Cf. T. M. Knox and Richard Kroner (eds. and trans.), Georg Wilhelm Friedrich Hegel: *Early Theological Writings,* "The Spirit of Christianity" (Chicago, 1948), p. 187.

[5] Cf. *Fear and Trembling,* p. 22.

[6] Cf. Chapter IV.

[7] In the notorious Leopold and Loeb case there was initially no reason to commit a "perfect" crime, but only to go through with the "thrill killing" regardless of the consequences for anyone, including the perpetrators of the deed. The fact that Leopold and Loeb struggled to avoid police detection and subsequently prosecution, in a way casts doubts on their ideological commitment. A true Nietzschean superman would not care what society did to him so long as he had been loyal to his particular values. Analogously, Raskolnikov must live with his own conscience even if the police should never discover his tracks. The "ideological" crime, it would appear, has two distinct facets to it. On the one hand, it entails fanatical devotion to a cause irrespective of consequences; on the other, and sometimes inconsistently, it requires "perfect" execution. In Raskolnikov's situation there are, correspondingly, two major issues: does he break down because Porfiry has seen through his disguises or, far more important, it seems to me, because he is unable to live with himself after the crime, his "flesh" in the Pauline sense being weaker than his ideology. *Crime and Punishment* is not primarily a detective story just as the Book of Job was not intended as a clinical treatise on human suffering. Had Raskolnikov been true to his philosophy, Inspector Porfiry could not really have bothered him. The very fact that he did so from the beginning underscores, I take

it, Dostoevsky's principal theme that man invites spiritual self-destruction by overstepping his limits. This helps make *Crime and Punishment* a genuine tragedy in addition to a unique psychological study.

⁸ *Crime and Punishment,* a new translation by David Magarshack (Harmondsworth, 1951), p. 557.

⁹ Sonia's redemption of Raskolnikov is the reverse of Liza's "failure" to save the Underground Man. Cf. Chapter V. A further revealing contrast characterizes the Captain in Conrad's *The Secret Sharer* and Captain Vere. Conrad's Captain deviates from duty and risks his life, his ship, and his reputation in order to give Leggatt, a convicted murderer, a new start in life. "I asked myself whether it was wise to interfere with the established routine of duties even from the kindest of motives," the Captain reflects. His affirmative response to this doubt clearly is a case of the "teleological suspension." By remaining true to himself the Captain saves not only Leggatt, his alter ego, but his own self as well.

VII. *The Breakdown of Romantic Enlightenment*

¹ *The Dehumanization of Art* in *The Dehumanization of Art and Other Writings on Art and Culture* (New York, 1956), p. 21.

² Cf. Franz Kafka, *Selected Short Stories,* tr. Willa and Edwin Muir (New York, 1952).

³ Ibid., "The Hunger Artist," p. 198.

⁴ Ibid., "The Burrow," p. 291.

⁵ Ibid., "Metamorphosis," pp. 76-7.

⁶ Ibid., "The Penal Colony," p. 109.

⁷ Ibid., "The Hunger Artist," p. 200.

⁸ Ibid., "The Burrow," p. 268.

⁹ Ibid., "The Penal Colony," p. 126.

¹⁰ Ibid., "The Penal Colony," p. 104.

¹¹ Ibid., "The Penal Colony," p. 126.

¹² Ibid., "The Burrow," p. 303.

¹³ Ibid., "The Penal Colony," p. 127.

¹⁴ Ibid., "The Hunger Artist," p. 201.

Conclusion

¹ *Memoirs of a Dutiful Daughter,* tr. James Kirkup (Cleveland and New York, 1959).

² Ibid., p. 207.

THE MERIDIAN

Twice yearly, in the spring and fall publishing seasons, Meridian Books take to newspaper format and issue *The Meridian,* a lively eight-page tabloid distributed free to thousands of subscribers. Its purpose, like that of any good house organ, is to acquaint readers with the present and future activities of the various imprints of the firm: Meridian Books, Meridian Giants, Living Age Books, Greenwich Editions, the Jewish Publication Society Series, Meridian Fiction, and Meridian Periodicals. The news is scattered in pre-publication reviews, selections from forthcoming books, guest features by authors, blurbs on projects vague and concrete—even in pictures. Among the standard features are the ever-popular "Tax Tips for the Teacher" and a complete list of all titles published by Meridian Books. For a free, unlimited subscription, write to:

The Meridian
12 East 22 Street
New York 10, New York

MERIDIAN BOOKS

12 East 22 Street, New York 10, New York

Titles listed here are **not** necessarily available in the British Empire

Meridian Fiction

12 East 22 Street, New York 10, New York

All Meridian Fiction publications are contemporary works of literary distinction deserving the broader readership made possible by paperback editions. They are printed on specially made Meridian Eggshell paper and Perfect Bound for durability.
MERIDIAN FICTION IS DISTRIBUTED BY MERIDIAN BOOKS, INC.

LIVING AGE BOOKS

published by MERIDIAN BOOKS, INC.

12 East 22 Street, New York 10, New York

Titles listed here are not necessarily available in the British Empire